Stock Market Profits
with
CONVERTIBLES

Stock Market Profits
with
CONVERTIBLES

by
Sidney Fried

RHM PRESS
a division of RHM Associates of Delaware, Inc.
840 Willis Avenue, Albertson, N.Y. 11507

Copyright © 1976
RHM PRESS
a division of RHM Associates of Delaware, Inc.
840 Willis Avenue, Albertson, N.Y. 11507

Library of Congress Cataloging in Publication Data
Fried, Sidney.
   Stock market profiits with convertibles.
   1. Convertible bonds.   2. Convertible preferred
stocks.   3. Speculation. I. Title.
HG6036.F74   332.6'323   74-17847
ISBN 0-89058-602-0

Printed in the United States of America

Other Books by the Author

Warrants PLUS Call Options PLUS Technical Analysis:
A Road to Stock Market Success

Sidney Fried is Editor of:
>The R.H.M. Convertible Survey
>The R.H.M. Survey of Warrants, Options & Low-Price Stocks

To Carolyn

Author's Foreword

Dear Reader:

For almost three decades, in many capacities, as financial analyst, professional trader, and for more than 20 years as Editor of a leading investment service, this writer has followed the world of the Convertible—the Convertible Bond and the Convertible Preferred Stock.

If we were to pick one observation to cover that entire period, we would relate it to the great numbers of missed opportunities throughout by the general investing public stemming from simple ignorance about what Convertibles are, and how they may be wisely used.

As the opening pages which follow quickly show, the deficiencies start with a throwing away of money—purely and simply! A Convertible is available which, at a minimum, will show exactly as much profit, dollar-for-dollar invested, as the common stock in a rising market, and cannot show any greater *loss* than this common stock. The Convertible has, say, a 7% yield, the common has a 0 yield. Why buy the common stock instead of the Convertible and throw away that 7% yield?

There are no hidden reasons making the purchase of the common instead of the Convertible somehow appropriate and reasonable. None whatever. Yet, in trading going on today, as you read these words, investors are throwing money away by the handful in exactly this area. And to our own knowledge, year after year, it is not only average investors who do this, but large investors as well who are quite sophisticated in many other phases of the securities market, and many, many professionals too!

In the book, we have chapter after chapter piling up the special plus factors which wise use of almost 1000 active Convertibles can confer upon any investor. From higher yields and lower commission costs we go to the diminished downside risk to one's capital which can flow from knowledgeable use of Convertibles. And these lower risk factors, when understood and correctly utilized, can then help any investor to, on the one hand, safeguard his capital near market tops, and on the other hand, to boldly seize profit opportunities at market bottoms when most other investors are standing timorously on the sidelines.

Sharpening the profit potential still further, we go to another chapter where that remarkable instrument, the Convertible Hedge, comes into play, where simultaneous Long Convertible, Short common stock positions can perform notable feats in maximizing profits and minimizing risks. Then on to the Convertible applications to the latest exploding phenomenon, the Option market, where the Convertible Hedge becomes the Long Convertible, Short Option to perform more profit magic.

Important tax advantages, improvement in market timing, a host of other benefits await the investor who is willing to devote part of his time to careful study of what Convertibles can do for him in virtually every phase of investment activity and goals.

We have had for our goal in the pages ahead, to take what we have learned in nearly thirty years of daily study of "Opportunities In Convertibles" and to shape it into understanding and guidance for you, the reader, in today's stock market. We feel strongly that whatever care and interest you now apply to absorbing the message of those pages can be turned into the pure gold of sharply improved performance for your investment funds.

Sidney Fried

A Note From The Publisher

After reading this book you will quite naturally wish to know:

(a) What Convertibles are trading in today's market;

(b) What are their applicable Conversion terms and other relevant statistical data;

(c) How the author rates these Convertibles on the basis of current stock market trends.

Since you are purchasing this book through a book store, there will naturally be an appreciable time lag between the author's manuscript and the time you take it off the bookshelf. Since, in the stock market, even one day's news and events can bulk large in the fortunes of an individual company and its securities, giving the above information and opinion of this writer in the categories described in the book itself would be of doubtful value, and perhaps even counterproductive, since the reader would be unaware of important changes that might have taken place for some of the Convertibles since the book's publication.

Consequently, since we have not placed that potentially dated material in the book itself, we are prepared to send Sidney Fried's current and updated analysis and statistical presentation, covering all the points described above, to each reader on request, and at no additional cost.

To receive this valuable material, you need only send your full name and address (be sure to include zip) to:

R.H.M. Press   Dept. 85
840 Willis Avenue
Albertson, Long Island
New York 11507

We thank you for the interest you have shown in this book.

R.H.M. Press

How Investors Injure Themselves By Simple Ignorance Of "Opportunities In Convertibles"—

And How They Ignore Some Of The Best Roads To Stock Market Success

It is early-April 1975 and sharply-depressed Pan American World Airways common stock is trading actively on the New York Stock Exchange at $4.

On the same New York Stock Exchange, there is trading a *senior security* of Pan American, a Bond, the 7½s of 1998. But this is no ordinary Bond. It is a *Convertible* Bond, with each $100 face value of Bond convertible into (exchangeable for) 14.286 shares of Pan American common stock any time the holder of the Bond wishes to make the exchange.

Now, with Pan American common selling at $4 on the New York Stock Exchange, 14.286 shares of that common stock must be worth 4 x 14.286 or $57.14. What shall we make of the fact that the Pan American Convertible 7½s of 1998 are *selling* on the New York Stock Exchange at that exact price, at 57⅛ for each $100 face value certificate?

Lesson No. 1 about Convertibles: When *any* Convertible is selling in the market at a price equal to the market value of the common stock for which it can be exchanged, that Convertible is selling at *Conversion Parity,* a most important term in understanding Convertibles.

And when *any* Convertible is selling at Conversion Parity, it *must* show at least as much percentage profit as the common stock on any upside move for the common stock and *cannot* show any greater percentage loss than that common stock if the common stock moves to the downside.

The Convertible "arithmetic" involved is quite simple—but most important—so let the reader pay careful attention to this first point because we will arrive quickly at a "more money in the pocket" conclusion affecting *every* investment program, on every level. And then we will go on from there to demonstrate so many important approaches to "Stock Market Profits With Convertibles" that the reader will regret not having been fully conversant with Convertible opportunities for all the preceding years, and determined not to make the same mistakes today and in the future.

The Upside

Pan American common doubles in price, going from 4 to 8. At 8, the 14.286 shares of common into which each $100 face value of Bond can be converted are worth 8 x 14.286 or 114.28, and the Convertible must sell at least at that price. It can sell higher, at a premium, but it cannot sell for less.

Our Convertible Bond has exactly doubled from 57⅛ to 114¼, just as the common stock exactly doubled from 4 to 8. And on *any* upside move, the Convertible must *always* at least match the percentage profit in the common, because it started at Conversion Parity, the market price of the Convertible equal to the market value of the common stock into which it could be converted at any time.

The Downside

Pan American common is halved in price from 4 to 2. At 2, the 14.286 shares of common into which each $100 face value of Bond can be converted are worth 2 x 14.286 or 28.57. *If* the Convertible Bond had fallen that far it would have been exactly halved from 57⅛ to 28½, just as the common stock was exactly halved from 4 to 2. And on *any* downside move, again because it started at Conversion Parity, the Convertible must *always* stop its decline at least at the same percentage loss as the common. It can, and very often does, show *less* loss, and we will get to that very important point shortly, but for the time being let us simply realize that it cannot show a *greater* loss.

Our Illuminating First Point

In early-April 1975, with Pan American common at 4 and the Pan American Convertible 7½s of 1998 at 57⅛, we have seen that each $1 invested in the Convertible Bond *must* show at least as much profit as the same $1 invested in the common stock on any *upside* move, and cannot show any greater percentage loss than the common on the *downside*.

Does this mean that there is no difference at all between each $1 invested in the common stock of Pan American and the same $1 invested in the Convertible Bond? By no means! The very first distinction we take up, and there will be many more vital ones to follow in later pages, highlights the necessity for watching for "Opportunities In Convertibles." Here is that important first distinction.

In April 1975, Pan American common was paying no dividend. Return on the common stock investment 0

9

In the same April 1975, with Pan American Convertible 7½s of 1998 selling at 57⅛, the return on the Convertible Bond investment was 13.12%

In April 1975, *many* more investors were buying the *common stock* of Pan American than were buying the Pan American Convertible Bond.

And every one of those investors buying the common stock was throwing a 13.12% yield out the window, to no purpose whatever.

They were throwing this money away, not out of a conscious decision to do so, but out of simple ignorance that a Convertible Bond was available for the same company which would give them this large advantage in return on their investment, without any offsetting disadvantages whatever.

There are almost one thousand Convertible Bonds and Convertible Preferred Stocks trading in today's market covering every segment of the stock market from speculative stocks to the top-grade blue chips. With so many Convertibles trading, each time you buy a common stock without first checking to see if there is a Convertible trading for the same company, you run the risk of making the same costly error we have just described with Pan American World Airways.

Going Further

It is obvious that even if taking advantage of such higher yields were the *only* objective in watching Convertibles carefully, it would be more than enough reason to do so, but we are only at the very *beginning* of explaining the profit paths that can be taken with well-situated Convertibles, and let us now continue in expanded detail with another example, along with some preliminary definitions.

The publisher, R.H.M. Press, has agreed to make available to the reader, at no extra charge, a Special Supplement, giving the author's current and completely updated analysis and statistical presentation of the entire list of currently outstanding Convertible Bonds and Convertible Preferred Stocks, including a statistical presentation of Euro-Convertible Bonds and Convertibles with Call Option Hedge Potential, in accordance with the description of these areas of "Opportunities In Convertibles" set forth in this book.

To receive this Special Supplement, important to following current opportunities, send your name and address—be sure to include zip—to:

R.H.M. Press Dept. 85
840 Willis Avenue
Albertson, Long Island
New York 11507

There will be no charge for this Special Supplement.

More Enlightenment

What IS A Convertible?

Convertible Bonds and Convertible Preferred Stocks are senior securities of a company, with all the attributes of "straight" (non-convertible) Bonds or Preferred Stocks, but also possessing, in addition to the usual rights and privileges of a senior security, the right to exchange (or "convert") the senior security into a specified number of shares of common stock, for a specified, and typically lengthy or perpetual, period of time.

The Example Of Gulf Resources &
Chemical Convertible Bonds

If we follow an additional example through, more relevant definitions of what constitutes "Opportunities in Convertibles" will fall quickly into place, buttressing what we just learned with the example of Pan American Convertible Bonds, and illuminating other important advantages of well-situated Convertibles.

It is late-November 1974, and Gulf Resources & Chemical common stock is selling on the New York Stock Exchange at 11⅛. With 1974 sales in the $250 million area, Gulf Resources mines lead, zinc, silver, cadmium, coal, lithium and other minerals. Despite substantial earnings, the depressed 1974 market has pushed the stock down to comparatively low levels, along with thousands of other common stocks.

On the same New York Stock Exchange, there is also trading another security—a *Convertible Bond* of Gulf Resources & Chemical. The Bond trades as the "6¼s of 1991," which means that each $100 face value Certificate pays interest of $6.25 per annum, and that in 1991, Gulf Resources will redeem the Bond from its then holder for $100 in cash. Bonds are quoted on the New York Stock Exchange (and other Exchanges) as well as over-the-counter in $100 units.

When a Bond sells for, say, 108¼, you pay $108.25 for each $100 face value of Bond. At that price, $6.25 in interest during the year comes to a yield of 5.77% (6.25 divided by 108.25). If, instead, the Bond is selling at, say, 84½, you now pay $84.50 for each $100 face value of Bond and the yield is 7.39% (6.25 divided by 84.50). The climbing effective yield on the Bond as the Bond drops in price in the marketplace is one of the major reasons for the Bond (or the Preferred Stock) beginning to drop more slowly than the common stock on a percentage basis after the strategic area for the common-Convertible price relationship is reached—and much more about this very vital and fundamental factor in later pages.

In that period of late-November 1974, with Gulf Resources & Chemical common selling at 11⅛, the Convertible 6¼s of 1991 were selling at 84½, and this price for the Bond takes on important significance when we come to the actual Conversion right of the Bond. Each $100 face value of Bond—irrespective of the market price of the Bond, whether at 108¼ or 84½ or any other price—was convertible into (exchangeable for) 7.587 shares of common stock, any time the holder of the Bond wished to make the exchange.

7.587 shares of Gulf Resources & Chemical common

stock, when that stock is selling in the open market at 11⅛ (11.125), are worth 7.587 x 11.125 or *84.41*.

Since the Convertible Bond was *selling* for 84½ ($84.50), almost exactly equal to the market value of the common stock for which it could be exchanged upon conversion, the *premium* over direct Conversion Value—another important term—is 0, and the Convertible Bond is selling at "Conversion Parity" as we have previously described.

Two Important Facts
Fact No. I

To repeat once more because of the importance of the concept, whenever a Convertible, *any* Convertible, is selling at Conversion Parity, each dollar invested in the Convertible *must* show at least as much percentage profit as the common stock if that common stock moves up.

The Convertible can show a *higher* profit than the common, selling at a premium over Conversion Value, but it cannot show a smaller profit, and we now again demonstrate this simple, but vital, concept by describing what actually happened to Gulf Resources & Chemical Convertible Bonds and common stock in the seven months following November 1974, this time using two alternative equal investments—A or B.

Investment (A) in the Common Stock: You purchased 380 shares of Gulf Resources & Chemical common stock at 11⅛ for a total investment of. . . . $4,227

Investment (B) in the Convertible Bond: You purchased $5,000 face amount of Gulf Resources & Chemical Convertible 6¼s of 1991 at 84½ for a total investment of $4,225

14

In late-May 1975, Gulf Resources & Chemical common stock reached a high of 25⅜. Therefore, the $4,227 invested in 380 shares of common stock at 11⅛, with the common stock now at 25⅜, was worth 380 x 25.375 or $9,642, a profit of $5,415, representing a gain of 128%

What is the effect on the holder of $5,000 face value of the Convertible Bond of Gulf Resources & Chemical, if the common stock moves from 11⅛ to 25⅜? Each $100 face value of the 6¼s of 1991 is convertible into 7.587 shares of common stock, so $5,000 face value is convertible into 50 times 7.587, or 380 shares, which are worth $9,642 with the common at 25⅜, a profit of $5,417 over the original investment in the Bond, a profit of 128%

The gain for Gulf Resources & Chemical Convertible Bonds had exactly equaled the gain for the common stock.

When Gulf Resources common moved up from 11¼ to 25⅜, then, between late-November 1975 to late-May 1975:

Investment (A) in the common stock showed a gain of 128%

and

Investment (B) in the Convertible Bond showed exactly the same gain of 128%

A little reflection will show that when *any* Convertible is selling at *Conversion Parity*, the market price of the Convertible equal to the market value of the common stock for which it can be exchanged, the Convertible *must* equal any advance in the common, dollar-for-dollar invested, because the Convertible senior security can be *exchanged* for that amount of common stock any time the holder of the Convertible wishes to make the exchange, just as we demonstrated with the rise in Gulf Resources & Chemical.

The holder of the Convertible does not even have to "convert" into the common to gain his profit, for the market price of the Convertible must move up as its Conversion Value moves up (professional arbitrageurs will see to that) allowing the profit to be taken by merely selling out one's Convertible position.

Fact No. II

Whenever a Convertible, *any* convertible, is selling at Conversion Parity, the market price of the Convertible equal to the market value of the number of shares of common stock into which it can be converted upon demand, and the common stock *declines* in price, the Convertible can *not* show a *greater* loss than the common stock, per dollar invested, but can, and very often does, show a *smaller* percentage loss than that endured by the common stock.

Once again, we can let the reality of actual market performance illustrate this vital point, and we can do this by looking at the market behavior of Gulf Resources & Chemical common and Convertible Bond in 1974 when, in the panicky and depressed markets of that year, Gulf Resources & Chemical common dropped to a low of 6¼.

Considering Investment (A)—the 380 shares of common purchased at 11⅛ for a total investment of $4,227—a return to the 1974 low of 6¼ would make the investment worth only 6.25 x 380 or *$2,375.*

Could Investment (B), the $5,000 face value of Convertible Bonds purchased at 84½ for a total investment of

$4,225, show a greater loss than the common stock, with the latter at the 1974 low of 6¼? No, this would not be possible. For, *at worst,* the $5,000 face value of Convertible Bond could be exchanged at any time for 380 shares of common stock, worth exactly the same $2,375 indicated above with the common at 6¼.

But reality dealt more kindly with the Convertible Bond at *its* low for 1974. Each $100 face value of Bond, which cost $84.50 remember, was convertible into 7.587 shares of common stock, and at 6¼ for the common, the Conversion Value of the Bond was 6.25 x 7.587 or 47.41 at the 1974 low.

Had the Convertible Bond dropped to 47.41, the $5,000 face amount of Bond would have been worth only $2,375, and the loss in the Convertible would indeed have equaled that for the common.

But at 47.41 the 6¼% Bond would have been yielding 13% and would still have possessed all the superior attributes of a "senior security" compared with the common (attributes we shall shortly describe). Because of these factors, Gulf Resources Convertible Bonds did *not* fall to 47.41 when the common stock fell to its 6¼ low. Instead, the Convertible sold no lower than *60.*

At the 1974 lows of 6¼ for the common, and 60 for the Convertible Bond, then, how would Investments (A) and (B) have compared?

(Computations continue on following page)

17

Investment (A) in the common stock would have seen the $4,227 investment in 380 shares of common at 11¼, decline to a worth of $2,375 with the common at 6¼, a loss of $1,852

Investment (B) in the Convertible Bond would have seen the $4,225 investment in $5,000 face value of the Bond at 84½, decline to a worth of $3,000 with the Bond at 60, a loss of only $1,225

Many Convertibles of higher investment grade than Gulf Resources hold up to an even greater degree compared with their common stocks than we have just described, and we shall soon be giving examples of this. It is a fact that *almost all* Convertibles hold up better than their common stocks during a significant decline, many of them *far* better. But let us now turn to some vital questions which will begin to substantially lift the curtain on understanding "Opportunities In Convertibles."

The Vital—And Enlightening—Questions

We have seen that a Convertible selling at Conversion Parity, the market price of the Convertible equal to the market price of the number of shares of common stock for which it can be exchanged upon demand,

(1) *must* show at least equal percentage advance with the common stock on any upside move;

(2) *cannot* show a greater percentage decline than the common stock on any downside move; and, indeed

(3) typically shows a *smaller*—often a *far* smaller—percentage decline than the common stock during a significant decline of the latter.

The Vital Question: If the same dollar investment in the Convertible must show at least as much upside gain as the common on the upside, but very often shows less loss than the common on the downside, why buy the common instead of the Convertible, and needlessly expose yourself to this greater risk of loss?

Put in terms of our example of Gulf Resources & Chemical in late-November 1974, with the common at 11⅛ and the Convertible Bond at 84½ (selling at Conversion Parity), why should anyone have purchased the common rather than the Convertible Bond? Yet, *many* more investors bought the common rather than the Convertible Bond, as a look at comparative volume of trading reveals, and as happens with so many similar Convertible-common relationships. And the reason that the more favorable investment is overlooked is that most investors simply lack sufficient information and understanding about Convertibles.

19

Still Greater Comparative Advantages Of The Well-Selected Convertible

1. In November 1974, Gulf Resources & Chemical *common stock* paid no dividend whatever.

2. Gulf Resources *Convertible Bonds,* the 6¼s of 1991, paid interest of *$6.25 annually per $100 face value of Bond.* Thus, to go back to our two alternatives:

(A) Buy 380 shares of Gulf Resources common at 11⅛; Cost $4,227 . . . . .Dividend Return—0

(B) Buy $5,000 face amount of Gulf Resources Convertible Bond at 84½;
Cost $4,225 . . . . .Interest Yield—7.4%

Even Further:

(A) If you buy 380 shares of Gulf Resources common at 11⅛ for a total cost of $4,227, you typically pay a total brokerage commission of $103.22

(B) If, instead, you buy the equivalent amount in the Gulf Resources Convertible Bond at 84½, or $5,000 face amount, for a total cost of $4,225, you typically pay a total brokerage commission of . . . .$ 37.50

Thus, it is quite clear that in late-November 1974, the investor who bought Gulf Resources & Chemical *common stock* instead of the *Convertible Bond:*

(1) needlessly exposed himself to a considerably greater risk to his capital on the downside, to no purpose whatever;

(2) accepted a 0 return on his investment by buying the common, losing the 7.4% yield which would have come with the Convertible; and

(3) paid almost 3 times as much in commission charges for the privilege of so injuring himself!

We will shortly get to the *greatest* benefits enjoyed by the investor knowledgeable in the uses of Convertibles, more important even than the benefits just enumerated, but first let us look at a few more examples to further emphasize the values inherent in well-situated Convertibles.

LTV Convertible Bonds

It is the week ending 11-15-74 and the common stock of LTV is selling on the New York Stock Exchange at 10½. Operating through three major subsidiaries, Jones & Laughlin Steel, Wilson & Company and LTV Aerospace, sales were at $4.75 billion and 1974 earnings would eventually come in at $8 per share (!), but against such breathtaking earnings for a stock selling at 10½ there was Long-Term Debt of $1.12 billion and interest charges and responsibility for maturing debt that could conceivably threaten the financial stability of the company. Hence the extremely low Price/Earnings ratio.

Along with the common stock selling at 10½, on the same New York Stock Exchange there is trading an LTV *Convertible Bond,* the 7½s of 1977, which are selling at *100.* Each $100 face value of the 7½s of 1977 is convertible into 9.524 shares of LTV common stock, the convertible privilege good through the maturity of the Bond in 1977.

9.524 shares of common at the market price of 10½ comes to a market value of 9.524 x 10.5 or 100. The Convertible Bond is *selling* at 100 and, therefore, is selling at direct Conversion Parity. Just as with the previous example of Gulf Resources & Chemical, or with any other similar Convertible/common price relationship, the LTV Convertible Bond *must* show at least as much percentage appreciation as LTV common stock on the upside. Demonstrating this, LTV common stock does indeed advance to a 1975 high of 19¾, up 88%.

What happens to the LTV Convertible Bond? Just as we know *must* happen, at a minimum, the LTV Convertible Bond is worth 188 with the common at 19¾ (9.524 x 19.75 equals 188) and that is where the Convertible Bond sells, producing the same 88% advance as the common.

LTV Common And Convertible On The DOWNside

The 1974 low for LTV common, and the behavior of the Convertible Bond as that common low was approached, once again emphasizes the superior protective ability of the well-situated Convertible on the downside. The 1974 common low was 7⅞, and at 7⅞ the straight Conversion Value of the Convertible Bond was 9.524 x 7.875 or 75.

Did the LTV Convertible Bond drop as low as 75? No, it did not, the actual low for the Convertible being 87 at the time the common hit its low, and even that was but a momentary low for the Convertible, which snapped back to the 90s on the first minor lift in the common.

This tells us once again that in mid-November 1974 the LTV Convertible Bond was a far better buy than LTV common. Selling at direct Conversion Parity, the Convertible Bond promised just as much appreciation as the common stock, dollar-for-dollar invested, if the common stock headed to the upside, but exposed the purchaser to considerably less capital loss if the common stock were to head to the downside.

Further, at 100 in November 1974, the Convertible Bond

22

was yielding 7½%, while the dividend return on LTV common was—0.

And the commission charges on buying (and selling) the common was about 3 times as great as purchasing an equal dollar amount of the Convertible Bond.

In mid-November 1974, then, the purchaser of LTV common stock was, with no offsetting advantages whatever, accepting greater risk to his capital, throwing away a 7½% yield, and paying three times the amount of commission to so injure himself. Once again, this was done out of sheer lack of knowledge of the availability of the LTV Convertible Bond, possessing all the advantages we have just enumerated.

Amerada-Hess Convertible Preferred Stock

Thus far we have discussed the examples of Convertible superiority through two Convertible *Bonds*. Let's turn now to a Convertible *Preferred Stock,* to demonstrate that the Convertible advantages are equally valid when a Convertible Preferred Stock is the medium of investment. We shall also reach back to another market period—1970 in this case—to illustrate the fact that the common/Convertible relationships remain the same in *any* market period, those which have passed and those which are directly ahead, because the relationships are logical and mathematical, and must work in one period exactly as they have worked in another period.

Just a few pages later, in discussing further why almost all well-situated Convertibles hold up so much better than their respective common stocks on the downside, we will be defining the Preferred Stock in a specific sense, but at this time let us concentrate simply on the favorable Convertible "arithmetic," with the fully correct understanding that Convertible Bonds and Convertible Preferred Stocks provide precisely the same advantages.

It is February 1970 and Amerada-Hess common is selling at 25⅛ on the New York Stock Exchange. Amerada-Hess is a large, integrated oil company whose stock moved past the 60 mark in 1969, but which was decimated, along with thousands of other stocks, in the 1970 plunge. On the same New York Stock Exchange another security of Amerada-Hess is trading—a Convertible Preferred Stock, paying $3.50 per share per annum in dividends, and therefore trading as the $3.50 Preferred. Each share of the $3.50 Preferred is convertible into 2.2 shares of Amerada-Hess

24

common without time limit, any time the holder of the Preferred wishes to make the exchange.

2.2 x 25.25 equals 55.55. The Convertible Preferred is selling at 55.50 and is, therefore, selling at Conversion Parity and *must* show at least as much gain as the common stock on the upside. The common stock does indeed advance to an exuberant 1971 recovery high of 71½, up 183%. Now, at 71½, the Conversion Value of the Convertible Preferred is 2.2 x 71.5 which equals 157.30, and the Convertible cannot sell below its Conversion Value. Amerada-Hess $3.50 Convertible Preferred actually sells at 157¾, up the same 183% as the common stock, demonstrating our point anew that purchased at Conversion Parity (or very close to it) a Convertible *must* move up as fast as the common if that is where the common is headed.

But suppose the common does not move *up,* but reverses its course and heads to the downside? Here we know, from our past analysis, that the Convertible cannot possibly show a *greater* loss than the common, dollar-for-dollar invested, but typically slows its decline and, as the common continues to decline, develops a premium over straight Conversion Value, the *size* of the premium measuring the all-important holding power of the Convertible on the downside.

In the case of Amerada-Hess, the common did not go down much further in 1970, went straight up in 1971, and stayed at higher price levels thereafter, so for some years there was not a good test of the holding power of the $3.50 Convertible Preferred on the downside. In 1974-1975, however, Amerada-Hess common literally plunged in the market crack-up of that period and sagged to a low of *15⅛*. The $3.50 Convertible Preferred had a straight Conversion

Value at that common price of 2.2 x 15.125 which equals 33.27. But at 33¼, the $3.50 Convertible Preferred Stock of Amerada-Hess would have been yielding 10.52% as well as still possessing its perpetual conversion privilege into a common stock which had many times proved its ability to produce sharp and extensive recoveries. Because of these factors principally, the Convertible Preferred did not sell as low as 33¼ but, instead, sold no lower than *42*.

Thus did the Amerada-Hess $3.50 Convertible Preferred affirm its excellent downside holding power in 1974-1975, highlighting the exceedingly promising position it had held in 1970 when its ability to enjoy just as much upside appreciation as the common stock was joined by the even more important attribute of being able to resist *decline* to a far better extent than the common stock. Joined with this valuable attribute was the advantage of *higher yield,* since, in the February 1970 period of our example, Amerada-Hess common was yielding only 1.2% at its market price of 25⅛, while the $3.50 Convertible Preferred was yielding *6.3%* at its market price of 55½. Add lower commission costs and one again will ask why an investor in February 1970 would buy Amerada-Hess *common* with its much greater downside risk, far lower yield and higher commission cost, rather than the $3.50 Convertible Preferred which had the advantage on every count. We come up, of course, with the same answer: those investors who purchased the common rather than the Convertible did not do so from choice, but out of a lack of knowledge of the remarkable superiority of the well-situated Convertible.

Following 1,000 Convertibles

We doubt that there can now be much doubt in the mind of any reader that one should not buy a common stock, *any* common stock, without first checking to see if there is a Convertible Bond or a Convertible Preferred Stock trading for the same company. If such a Convertible *is* trading, and if that Convertible is selling at or near Conversion Parity, then it is more than possible that buying the Convertible rather than the common will give us the same profits, with much greater safety to invested capital and, very often, a higher yield, and, almost always, lower commission rates to buy and to sell.

In addition to these important points, we will shortly be getting to those Convertible attributes which we consider to be the most important, to lead to the most profit-producing avenues of the Convertible, but in view of the fact that the necessity of following the total Convertible picture has already been demonstrated even with the advantages thus far outlined, we must deal with the question: How do you *follow* 1,000 Convertibles?

When we first asked ourselves this question, there were not 1,000 Convertibles, but rather about 200. It was back in the late 1940's when we were at a trading desk for a securities firm and developing a special interest in all Convertible securities, such as *Warrants,* as well as Convertible Bonds and Convertible Preferred Stocks. Then there were "Put and Call Options," which had a special relationship to Convertibles which were to assume very large importance and considerable profit potential 30 years later when a new Call Option market sprang into prominence.

27

Where Convertibles were specifically concerned, we developed our own method of following them for the special needs of a trading desk and we soon took our ideas "public" by writing articles for The Commercial & Financial Chronicle in 1950 and publishing the first full-length treatment of the subject we are aware of, in a book entitled *Investment & Speculation In CONVERTIBLE Bonds & Preferreds.*

The book also appeared in 1950 and in the years that followed sold enough copies to generate additional interest in Convertibles among investors. Other factors also entered to spur the number of new Convertibles and, noting this increasing interest, investment bankers were happy to provide more such issues to supply investors' appetites, and the number of Convertible issues began to multiply beyond the ability of our initial methods of computation to follow Convertible opportunities.

In 1956, this writer became the Editor of the first investment service to devote itself entirely to Convertible Bonds and Convertible Preferred Stocks, first on a twice-monthly basis, and then on a weekly basis. That investment service was called The R.H.M. Convertible Survey, published by R.H.M. Associates, and this writer is still the Editor of that same Survey today, about 20,000 pages of Convertible computation and analysis later!

Our first statistical approach to following Convertibles was not much different from the one we are still following today, but the computations were originally done by a battery of Friden Electric Calculators, necessitating a clattering din for an entire day, and the chore of then typing and proofreading thousands of statistics to get ready for the printing press. Going on a computer was made to order for this mountainous task, and soon the thousands of calculations were being done in a few seconds, after which the entire section was turned out by the computer's high-speed print-out ready for the press.

It was fortunate indeed that the computer was able to take over the statistical job since the few hundred Convertibles were to become 1,000 Convertibles by the late-1960's.

Our Weekly Statistical Approach To Following Convertibles

For about ten years, 1956 to 1966, our R.H.M. Convertible Survey was the only investment service intensively covering the entire Convertibles field, apart from a few aborted attempts by some financial organizations in the early 1960's and, today, there are a few additional services also covering this field. With each of those services using basically the same computation methods we began with in 1956, describing the R.H.M. Survey's computer printout method of following 1,000 Convertibles will also serve to adequately describe these other approaches, at least in the basic statistical work.

Since the computer printout of the R.H.M. Convertible Survey measures about nine inches across, and is therefore printed the "long" way in the weekly Survey issues, we have cut the presentation into three parts, as depicted on the following pages. (Page 31 shows the full table reduced.) We will be keeping those three sections in front of the reader on each page as we take up the significance of the tables, column-by-column.

To visualize the complete presentation, conceive the two sections on the left- and right-hand pages to be joined together without a break *(A&B)*, as indeed they are in the normal presentation. And the smaller portion at the lower part of the right-hand page *(C)*, should be conceived of as being joined to the portion on the upper part of the right-hand page, without any break. In other words, it is really one complete statistical presentation without being chopped into three parts, but we have had to present it in this manner because of the space requirements.

Layout markers: **A** | **B** | **C**

Group Rating Tdd	Com-Bd.	Outst'g (Mill $)	ISSUE	Rate (%)	Mat.	Conv. Price ($)	Conv. Rate (Shares)	Yr. Conv. Exp.	Price Com.	Price Bond.	Common Conv. Value	Prem. C/V (%)	ESL	Ind. Common Div'd	Yield	Cur. Bond Yield	Notes (Last Page)
S-S		29.2	AMF INC	4.250	81	57.11	1.751	TO MAT	21.8	84.0	38.2	120		1.24	5.7	5.1	
S-S		8.8	APL CORP	5.750	88	13.55	7.380	TO MAT	16.6	121.0	122.5	0		1.00	6.0	4.8	
S-S		40.0	ARA SERVICES INC	4.625	96	101.33	.587	TO MAT	56.5	73.1	55.8	31	49	1.06	6.3	6.3	
S-S		25.0	A-T-O INC	4.375	87	58.50	1.709	TO MAT	9.5	56.0	16.2	246		.24	2.5	7.8	
A-O		2.9	ABERDEEN MANUFACTURING	5.875	88	12.97	7.710	TC MAT	8.3	62.5	64.0	94.1	16	.40	5.7	9.4	2
A-O		2.5	ADVANCED MEMORY SYSTEMS	8.000	91	8.82	11.338	TC MAT	8.3	94.5	94.1	0		.00	.0	8.5	
A-A		29.9	AIR REDUCTION	3.875	87	31.25	3.200	TC MAT	22.5	84.0	73.3	15	48	1.00	4.4	4.6	23
A-A		31.8	ALASKA AIRLINES	6.500	88	6.62	15.106	TC MAT	5.5	93.0	83.1	12		.00	.0	7.3	
A-A		1.8	ALASKA AIRLINES	6.875	87	7.52	13.295	TC MAT	5.5	82.0	73.1	12		.00	.0	8.4	
S-S		7.8	ALASKA INTERSTATE	6.000	96	26.00	3.846	TC MAT	15.1	77.8	58.1	36		.15	1.3	7.6	
S-S		20.0	ALEXANDERS INC	5.500	96	32.25	3.100	TC MAT	8.0	58.5	24.8	136		.80	1.3	9.4	
O-O		3.0	ALISON MORTGAGE INV TR	6.000	91	27.50	3.636	TC MAT	1.1	23.5	3.5	488		.0	.0	10.0	
A-A		15.0	ALLEGHENY AIRLINES	5.750	93	23.16	4.317	TC MAT	6.3	82.0	27.2	102		.00	.0	10.5	
O-O		10.2	ALLEGHENY BEVERAGE	6.250	88	8.72	11.468	TC MAT	2.7	50.5	31.0	63		.00	.0	12.4	1
S-S		5.7	ALLEGHENY LUDLUM IND	4.500	81	65.60	1.523	TC MAT	34.6	66.5	66.5	23		1.80	5.2	4.9	
O-O		5.9	ALLEN GROUP INC	6.000	94	14.00	7.143	TC MAT	13.3	115.5	95.0	22		.50	3.8	10.0	
A-A		1.6	ALLEN GROUP INC	6.000	87	23.54	4.246	TO MAT	13.3	64.0	66.5	13		.50	3.8	9.4	
A-A		2.8	ALLIED ARTISTS INDUSTRIES	8.750	90	2.25	44.444	TO MAT	1.4	78.0	62.2	25		.00	.0	11.2	
A-A		3.4	ALLIED STORES	4.500	81	3.571	28.00	TO MAT	46.1	172.0	164.6	5	59	1.70	2.6	2.6	
S-S		49.2	ALLIED STORES	4.500	92	44.50	2.247	TO MAT	46.1	105.0	95.0	22		1.70	3.7	4.3	
S-S		19.5	ALLIED SUPERMARKETS	5.750	87	15.44	6.477	TO MAT	3.3	47.0	21.4	120	49	1.70	3.7	4.3	
A-A		125.0	ALTEC CORP	15.000	95	1.20	83.333	TO MAT	1.3	110.5	108.3	2		.00	.0	12.2	
S-A		14.3	ALUMINUM COMPANY OF AMERICA	5.250	91	56.00	1.786	TO MAT	46.9	95.1	83.8	14	59	1.34	2.9	13.6	
A-A		12.0	AMERACE CORP	5.000	92	37.00	2.703	MAT	19.4	66.5	52.4	27	53	1.20	6.2	7.5	
S-S		167.0	AMERICAN AIR FILTER	6.000	90	26.50	3.774	MAT	19.0	94.0	71.7	31		.48	2.5	6.4	
S-S		9.8	AMERICAN AIRLINES	4.250	92	44.25	2.260	1-80	11.4	48.5	25.8	88		.00	.0	8.8	
S-A		2.4	AMERICAN AIRLINES	6.750	91	28.00	3.571	1-80	11.4	36.1	40.0	464		.00	.0	18.7	
S-S		12.0	AMERICAN CENTURY MTG INV	7.000	90	21.00	4.762	MAT	1.8	40.0	8.6	365		.00	.0	17.5	
O-O		15.0	AMERICAN CONTINENTAL HOMES	7.000	91	10.75	5.302	MAT	1.8	39.0	13.0	200		.00	.0	17.9	
O-O		17.9	AMERICAN EXPORT INDUSTRIES	5.250	93	57.00	1.754	MAT	.8	26.5	1.4	1793		.00	.0	19.8	
O-O		13.6	AMERICAN FINANCIAL CORP	5.500	88	12.04	8.306	MAT	6.6	61.5	54.8	12		.16	2.4	8.9	
S-S		55.0	AMERICAN GENERAL INSURANCE	6.500	94	40.00	2.500	12-79	38.1	103.5	95.3	8		1.00	2.6	6.3	48
S-S		4.4	AMERICAN HOIST & DERRICK	4.750	92	15.66	6.386	MAT	16.1	104.0	102.8	1		.80	5.0	4.6	
S-S		18.0	AMERICAN HOIST & DERRICK	5.500	93	20.87	4.792	MAT	16.1	82.3	77.2	7		.80	5.0	6.7	

Group/Rating side markers: 3H, 4, 5H, 3H, 5H, 3H, 3, 3, 3H, 3H, 5H, 3, 5H

Group Rating	Tdd Com-Bd.	Outst'g (Mill $)	ISSUE	Rate (%)
	S-S	29.2	AMF INC	4.250
3H	S-S	8.8	APL CORP	5.750
4	S-S	40.0	ARA SERVICES INC	4.625
	S-S	25.0	A-T-O INC	4.375
	A-O	2.9	ABERDEEN MANUFACTURING	5.875
	O-O	2.5	ADVANCED MEMORY SYSTEMS	8.000
3H	S-S	29.9	AIR REDUCTION	3.875
	A-A	31.8	ALASKA AIRLINES	6.500
5H	A-A	1.8	ALASKA AIRLINES	6.875
	S-S	7.8	ALASKA INTERSTATE	6.000
	S-S	20.0	ALEXANDERS INC	5.500

The "Permanent" Programming Section

Group Rating

Starting from the extreme left, we find the first column headed "Group Rating," and this has reference to this writer's weekly evaluation, as Editor, of the specific Convertible as an actual recommendation for "Buy," "Sell," "Hold" or "Hedge." The "Group Rating" column being a part of the actual investment service, we shall not be going into that further at this point, although a description of the investment service can be obtained by writing the R.H.M. Convertible Survey, 220 Fifth Avenue, New York, N.Y. 10001.

Tdd Com-Bd

Continuing our discussion of the computer printout, the second column is headed "Tdd Com-Bd." with the drastic abbreviations necessitated by the narrow width of that specific column. Spelled out, that heading refers to "Traded"

Mat.	CONVERSION Price ($)	Rate (Shares)	Yr. Conv. Exp.	PRICE Com.	Bond.	Common Conv. Value	Prem. C/V (%)

CONVERTIBLE BONDS

Mat.	Price	Rate	Exp.	Com.	Bond.	Value	Prem.
81	57.11	1.751 TO MAT	81	21.8	84.0	38.2	120
88	13.55	7.380 TO MAT	88	16.6	121.0	122.5	0
96	101.33	.987 TO MAT	96	56.5	73.1	55.8	31
87	58.50	1.709 TO MAT	87	9.5	56.0	16.2	246
88	12.97	7.710 TO MAT	88	7.0	62.5	54.0	16
91	8.82	11.338 TO MAT	91	8.3	94.5	94.1	0
87	31.25	3.200 TO MAT	87	22.9	84.0	73.3	15
86	6.62	15.106 TO MAT	86	5.5	93.0	83.1	12
87	7.52	13.299 TO MAT	87	5.5	82.0	73.1	12
96	26.00	3.846 TO MAT	96	15.1	78.8	58.1	36
96	32.25	3.100 TO MAT	96	8.0	58.5	24.8	136

ESL	INDICATED COMMON Div'd	Yield	Cur. Bond Yield	Notes (Last Page)
	1.24	5.7	5.1	
	1.00	6.0	4.8	
49	1.06	1.9	6.3	
	.24	2.5	7.8	
	.40	5.7	9.4	2
	.00	.0	8.5	
48	1.00	4.4	4.6	23
	.00	.0	7.0	
	.00	.0	8.4	
	.15	1.0	7.6	
	.10	1.3	9.4	

and "Common-Bond" (and in another section covering Convertible Preferred Stocks to "Common-Preferred Stock") and tells us where each of the issues is being traded. This is given in Common-Convertible order, the first letter denoting

33

Group Rating	Tdd Com·Bd.	Outst'g (Mill $)	ISSUE	Rate (%)
	S-S	29.2	AMF INC	4.250
3H	S-S	8.8	APL CORP	5.750
4	S-S	40.0	ARA SERVICES INC	4.625
	S-S	25.0	A-T-O INC	4.375
	A-O	2.9	ABERDEEN MANUFACTURING	5.875
	O-O	2.5	ADVANCED MEMORY SYSTEMS	8.000
3H	S-S	29.9	AIR REDUCTION	3.875
	A-A	31.8	ALASKA AIRLINES	6.500
5H	A-A	1.8	ALASKA AIRLINES	6.875
	S-S	7.8	ALASKA INTERSTATE	6.000
	S-S	20.0	ALEXANDERS INC	5.500

where the common stock is being traded, and the second letter where the Convertible is being traded.

The various designations are "S" for New York Stock Exchange, "A" for American Stock Exchange, "O" for over-the-counter, "P" for Pacific Coast Exchange, and "M" for Midwest Stock Exchange. "S-S" would indicate that both common and Convertible are trading on the New York Stock Exchange; "S-O" would indicate that the common stock is trading on the New York Stock Exchange, and that the Convertible is trading over-the-counter. And so on. Almost all the important Convertibles, and their common stocks, are to be found trading on the New York Stock Exchange.

Outst'g (Mill $)

Here the size of the outstanding face amount of the Convertible Bond issue is given in millions of dollars. Thus, if we see "14.3" in this column, it means that $14,300,000 in

Mat.	CONVERSION Price ($)	CONVERSION Rate (Shares)		Yr. Conv. Exp.	PRICE Com.	PRICE Bond.	Common Conv. Value	Prem. C/V (%)

CONVERTIBLE BONDS

Mat.	Price ($)	Rate (Shares)		Yr. Conv. Exp.	Com.	Bond.	Common Conv. Value	Prem. C/V (%)
81	57.11	1.751	TO MAT	81	21.8	84.0	38.2	120
88	13.55	7.380	TO MAT	88	16.6	121.0	122.5	0
96	101.33	.987	TO MAT	96	56.5	73.1	55.8	31
87	58.50	1.709	TO MAT	87	9.5	56.0	16.2	246
88	12.97	7.710	TO MAT	88	7.0	62.5	54.0	16
91	8.82	11.338	TO MAT	91	8.3	94.5	94.1	0
87	31.25	3.200	TO MAT	87	22.9	84.0	73.3	15
86	6.62	15.106	TO MAT	86	5.5	93.0	83.1	12
87	7.52	13.299	TO MAT	87	5.5	82.0	73.1	12
96	26.00	3.846	TO MAT	96	15.1	78.8	58.1	36
96	32.25	3.100	TO MAT	96	8.0	58.5	24.8	136

ESL	INDICATED COMMON Div'd	INDICATED COMMON Yield	Cur. Bond Yield	Notes (Last Page)
	1.24	5.7	5.1	
	1.00	6.0	4.8	
49	1.06	1.9	6.3	
	.24	2.5	7.8	
	.40	5.7	9.4	2
	.00	.0	8.5	
48	1.00	4.4	4.6	23
	.00	.0	7.0	
	.00	.0	8.4	
	.15	1.0	7.6	
	.10	1.3	9.4	

face value is outstanding. When we get to the Convertible Preferred Stock section, this column becomes "Outst'g (000 Shs.)" and refers then to the number of shares of preferred stock outstanding in that particular Convertible issue, given

Group Rating	Tdd Com-Bd.	Outst'g (Mill $)	ISSUE	Rate (%)
	S–S	29.2	AMF INC	4.250
3H	S–S	8.8	APL CORP	5.750
4	S–S	40.0	ARA SERVICES INC	4.625
	S–S	25.0	A-T-O INC	4.375
	A–O	2.9	ABERDEEN MANUFACTURING	5.875
	O–O	2.5	ADVANCED MEMORY SYSTEMS	8.000
3H	S–S	29.9	AIR REDUCTION	3.875
	A–A	31.8	ALASKA AIRLINES	6.500
5H	A–A	1.8	ALASKA AIRLINES	6.875
	S–S	7.8	ALASKA INTERSTATE	6.000
	S–S	20.0	ALEXANDERS INC	5.500

in thousands of shares. If we see "1070.0" in that column, it refers to 1,070,000 shares of Convertible Preferred Stock outstanding in that particular issue.

The size of the issue is an important guide as to how much active trading we can expect, how good "the market" will be in that issue.

Issue, Rate, Maturity

Here we have the actual "name" of the security as it is traded. Thus, the AMF Inc. 4¼s of 1981 would find the company's name under the "Issue" heading, the 4.250 (4¼) under "Rate (%)" and the 81 (1981) under "Mat."

"Rate" is the amount of interest paid annually on each $100 face value of Bond. When we get to the Convertible Preferred Stock section, this column becomes "Div." referring to the annual dividend paid per share of stock.

"Mat." refers to the year in which the Bond matures, each $100 face value of Bond then being redeemed by the

CONVERTIBLE BONDS

Mat.	Conversion Price ($)	Conversion Rate (Shares)	Yr. Conv. Exp.	Price Com.	Price Bond.	Common Conv. Value	Prem. C/V (%)	ESL	Indicated Common Div'd	Indicated Common Yield	Cur. Bond Yield	Notes (Last Page)
81	57.11	1.751 TO MAT	81	21.8	84.0	38.2	120		1.24	5.7	5.1	
88	13.55	7.380 TO MAT	88	16.6	121.0	122.5	0		1.00	6.0	4.8	
96	101.33	.987 TO MAT	96	56.5	73.1	55.8	31	49	1.06	1.9	6.3	
87	58.50	1.709 TO MAT	87	9.5	56.0	16.2	246		.24	2.5	7.8	
88	12.97	7.710 TO MAT	88	7.0	62.5	54.0	16		.40	5.7	9.4	2
91	8.82	11.338 TO MAT	91	8.3	94.5	94.1	0		.00	.0	8.5	
87	31.25	3.200 TO MAT	87	22.9	84.0	73.3	15	48	1.00	4.4	4.6	23
86	6.62	15.106 TO MAT	86	5.5	93.0	83.1	12		.00	.0	7.0	
87	7.52	13.299 TO MAT	87	5.5	82.0	73.1	12		.00	.0	8.4	
96	26.00	3.846 TO MAT	96	15.1	78.8	58.1	36		.15	1.0	7.6	
96	32.25	3.100 TO MAT	96	8.0	58.5	24.8	136		.10	1.3	9.4	

company at full face value. This does not appear in the columns covering Convertible Preferred Stock, since no maturity date is involved. Instead, we have a column headed "Par" which refers to the "Par Value" of the Preferred

Group Rating	Tdd Com-Bd.	Outst'g (Mill $)	ISSUE	Rate (%)
	S–S	29.2	AMF INC	4.250
3H	S–S	8.8	APL CORP	5.750
4	S–S	40.0	ARA SERVICES INC	4.625
	S–S	25.0	A–T–O INC	4.375
	A–O	2.9	ABERDEEN MANUFACTURING	5.875
	O–O	2.5	ADVANCED MEMORY SYSTEMS	8.000
3H	S–S	29.9	AIR REDUCTION	3.875
	A–A	31.8	ALASKA AIRLINES	6.500
5H	A–A	1.8	ALASKA AIRLINES	6.875
	S–S	7.8	ALASKA INTERSTATE	6.000
	S–S	20.0	ALEXANDERS INC	5.500

Stock. There is no need to get into the meaning or lack of meaning of the term "Par Value" (it doesn't have much meaning) and let us treat it merely as another part of the "name" of the issue, allowing us to identify it readily, particularly when there are a number of Preferred Stock issues outstanding for a company.

Conversion, Price And Rate

This is one of the important focal points of the computer operation, telling us how many shares of common stock each $100 face value of Convertible is convertible into.

"Price" refers to the original issuance of the Convertible Bond, when the Conversion Rate is stated in dollars to give it some meaningful relationship to the price of the common stock at that time. Thus, a company's Prospectus for a Convertible Bond issue may state that the Bond is convertible at "$65 per share." Another way of stating that is to say that at 65 for the common stock, the number of shares into

Mat.	CONVERSION Price ($)	Rate (Shares)		Yr. Conv. Exp.	PRICE Com.	Bond.	Common Conv. Value	Prem. C/V (%)

CONVERTIBLE BONDS

Mat.	Price ($)	Rate (Shares)		Yr. Conv. Exp.	Com.	Bond.	Common Conv. Value	Prem. C/V (%)
81	57.11	1.751	TO MAT	81	21.8	84.0	38.2	120
88	13.55	7.380	TO MAT	88	16.6	121.0	122.5	0
96	101.33	.987	TO MAT	96	56.5	73.1	55.8	31
87	58.50	1.709	TO MAT	87	9.5	56.0	16.2	246
88	12.97	7.710	TC MAT	88	7.0	62.5	54.0	16
91	8.82	11.338	TO MAT	91	8.3	94.5	94.1	0
87	31.25	3.200	TC MAT	87	22.9	84.0	73.3	15
86	6.62	15.106	TO MAT	86	5.5	93.0	83.1	12
87	7.52	13.299	TO MAT	87	5.5	82.0	73.1	12
96	26.00	3.846	TO MAT	96	15.1	78.8	58.1	36
96	32.25	3.100	TO MAT	96	8.0	58.5	24.8	136

ESL	INDICATED COMMON Div'd	Yield	Cur. Bond Yield	Notes (Last Page)
	1.24	5.7	5.1	
	1.00	6.0	4.8	
49	1.06	1.9	6.3	
	.24	2.5	7.8	
	.40	5.7	9.4	2
	.00	.0	8.5	
48	1.00	4.4	4.6	23
	.00	.0	7.0	
	.00	.0	8.4	
	.15	1.0	7.6	
	.10	1.3	9.4	

which each $100 face value of Bond is convertible, gives
that $100 Bond a Conversion Value of 100.

This leads directly into "Rate," which is the specific number of shares into which each $100 face value of Bond is

Group Rating	Tdd Com-Bd.	Outst'g (Mill $)	ISSUE	Rate (%)
	S-S	29.2	AMF INC	4.250
3H	S-S	8.8	APL CORP	5.750
4	S-S	40.0	ARA SERVICES INC	4.625
	S-S	25.0	A-T-O INC	4.375
	A-O	2.9	ABERDEEN MANUFACTURING	5.875
	O-O	2.5	ADVANCED MEMORY SYSTEMS	8.000
3H	S-S	29.9	AIR REDUCTION	3.875
	A-A	31.8	ALASKA AIRLINES	6.500
5H	A-A	1.8	ALASKA AIRLINES	6.875
	S-S	7.8	ALASKA INTERSTATE	6.000
	S-S	20.0	ALEXANDERS INC	5.500

convertible. "Rate" is derived by dividing "Price" into 100. For example, if the "Price" is 65, dividing 65 into 100 gives us 1.538, and we stop at three decimal points to respond to the needs of the computer.

Restating this concept, if the common stock were to sell at 65, each $100 Bond would have a Conversion Value of 65 x 1.538, which, of course is 100.

The "Rate" column also tells us for how many years the conversion privilege runs. In the great majority of cases, this is stated as "TO MAT" which means to the maturity of the Bond, given under that column as previously described. Typically, this is 5, 10, 15 and 20 years, depending mostly upon when the Convertible Bond was first issued. In a few cases, a more restricted conversion life holds true. Thus, the Standard-Pacific Corp. 8½s of 1981 see their conversion privilege expire in October 1976 even though the Bond does not mature until 1981. Obviously, careful attention must be paid to such shortened conversion privileges, but

Mat.	CONVERSION Price ($)	CONVERSION Rate (Shares)	Yr. Conv. Exp.	PRICE Com.	PRICE Bond.	Common Conv. Value	Prem. C/V (%)

CONVERTIBLE BONDS

Mat.	Price ($)	Rate (Shares)			Yr. Exp.	Com.	Bond.	Value	C/V (%)
81	57.11	1.751	TO	MAT	81	21.8	84.0	38.2	120
88	13.55	7.380	TO	MAT	88	16.6	121.0	122.5	0
96	101.33	.987	TO	MAT	96	56.5	73.1	55.8	31
87	58.50	1.709	TO	MAT	87	9.5	56.0	16.2	246
88	12.97	7.710	TO	MAT	88	7.0	62.5	54.0	16
91	8.82	11.338	TO	MAT	91	8.3	94.5	94.1	0
87	31.25	3.200	TO	MAT	87	22.9	84.0	73.3	15
86	6.62	15.106	TO	MAT	86	5.5	93.0	83.1	12
87	7.52	13.299	TO	MAT	87	5.5	82.0	73.1	12
96	26.00	3.846	TO	MAT	96	15.1	78.8	58.1	36
96	32.25	3.100	TO	MAT	96	8.0	58.5	24.8	136

ESL	INDICATED COMMON Div'd	INDICATED COMMON Yield	Cur. Bond Yield	Notes (Last Page)
	1.24	5.7	5.1	
	1.00	6.0	4.8	
49	1.06	1.9	6.3	
	.24	2.5	7.8	
	.40	5.7	9.4	2
	.00	.0	8.5	
48	1.00	4.4	4.6	23
	.00	.0	7.0	
	.00	.0	8.4	
	.15	1.0	7.6	
	.10	1.3	9.4	

they are few in number among the 1,000 Convertibles, and whenever there is a shortened conversion privilege, prior to actual maturity, this is spelled out in this column.

Quite a number of Convertible Preferred Stock issues do

41

have expiration dates, even though the majority of them are perpetual and have no expiration date unless they are "Called," a term which we will deal with in a later chapter. Where there are expiration dates for the conversion privilege of a Convertible Preferred Stock, this is given in the computer printout next to "Rate."

Yr. Conv. Exp.

This column is a "reminder" column for the important information of the expiration date of the conversion privilege. It simply restates the year of such conversion privilege expiration.

| ESL | INDICATED COMMON | | Cur. Bond | Notes (Last |
	Div'd	Yield	Yield	Page)
	1.24	5.7	5.1	
	1.00	6.0	4.8	
49	1.06	1.9	6.3	
	.24	2.5	7.8	
	.40	5.7	9.4	2
	.00	.0	8.5	
48	1.00	4.4	4.6	23
	.00	.0	7.0	
	.00	.0	8.4	
	.15	1.0	7.6	
	.10	1.3	9.4	

ESL

There remain three additional columns on the right hand section of the computer printout which are also part of the permanent computer program. The first of these is very important, and is headed "ESL," which stands for Estimated Support Level. Let us immediately state that the factor must represent, in considerable part, the *judgment* of the analyst. Prepared by this writer for the weekly issues of the R.H.M. Convertible Survey, this figure gives the judgment of the writer, as Editor of the Survey, as to where a specific Convertible will approximately cease to decline in price if a severe and sustained sinking spell were to hit the common stock.

In the pages to follow shortly, we will be dealing with the question of "Why Senior Securities—Bonds and Preferred Stocks—Hold Up Better Than Their Respective Common Stocks On The Downside." Part of the answer to that question is the status of these entities *as* senior securities, entitled to their full stated interest and dividend payments *before* the common stock can get anything at all, and having a claim to all assets of the company ahead of the common stock if the company, for any reason, goes into dissolution.

The worth of such superior characteristics in downside safety is typically referred to as the *"Investment Value"* of a Convertible senior security, or the price at which it would sell if it were *non*convertible and had to depend strictly on its investment merits as a senior security. This price is normally a function of safety of principal, amount of yield and the general level of interest rates and we will be going into these factors in detail in the next section. For the time being, however, let us realize that such major financial research organizations as Standard & Poor's and Moody's analyze and *rate* senior securities on the basis of their investment worth, which rating has quite a bit to do with where a senior security will sell. Thus, an "AA" bond with a 7% coupon may be selling at 85 at a particular period to yield 8.23%, and *all* "AA" bonds will probably be found selling somewhere near that same 8.23% yield area.

A *Convertible* Bond rated "AA" would then, presumably, begin to hold up at about an 8.23% yield if the common stock started plummeting, and this is why analysts interested in Convertibles pay attention to the senior securities Ratings of Standard & Poor's and Moody's and justifiably so.

But many analysts *stop* at such Ratings, and we think one can do much better in arriving at a meaningful and useful downside holding point for a convertible senior security by *also* taking into account *the worth of the continuing conversion privilege.* The need for this additional analysis is based on the indisputable fact that few Convertibles decline all the way down to their straight investment values as senior securities. Where their Standard & Poor's rating might call for them to sell at, for example, 75, we might find them selling no lower than *85*. Where do the extra 10 points of value come from? From the value placed on the continuing conversion privilege, of course. Thus, XYZ 6½% Convertible Bonds may be rated "A" by Standard & Poor's, which might entitle it, on straight investment value, to stop declining around the 78 level when XYZ common slides down a market toboggan, and Conversion Value is no longer there to support the Convertible Bond.

Instead of selling at 78, however, the fact that the XYZ 6½% Convertible Bonds are the right, say, to convert into 3.284 shares of XYZ common per $100 face value of Bond until *1988* enters the picture, and with complete justification since such a long-term conversion privilege obviously has value. Rather than selling at the straight investment value of all other 6½% "A"-rated nonconvertible Bonds, or at 78, the XYZ *Convertible* Bond might sell at 85, the additional 7 points being the value placed by investors on the continuing conversion privilege to 1988.

In deriving an "Estimated Support Level," this writer takes into account (a) the current Investment Value, reflecting the Ratings of the major services, (b) the history of the Convertible security—where it has ceased to decline in previous common stock slides of the past few years, and (c) our expectations for where the general level of interest rates might be moving in the immediate future. In the end, the "Estimated Support Level" figure we prescribe for each Convertible must contain a generous amount of this writer's *judgment,* particularly as regards money market movement over the months to come. But as a rough guide to where a Convertible senior security may be expected to stop declining when it loses the support of straight Conversion Value in a serious common stock decline, "Estimated Support Level," as we have described it, is much more useful, in this writer's opinion, than merely the straight Investment Value. This will, doubtless, become clearer as our analysis continues in chapters following.

Group Rating	Tdd Com-Bd.	Outst'g (Mill $)	ISSUE	Rate (%)
	S-S	29.2	AMF INC	4.250
3H	S-S	8.8	APL CORP	5.750
4	S-S	40.0	ARA SERVICES INC	4.625
	S-S	25.0	A-T-O INC	4.375
	A-O	2.9	ABERDEEN MANUFACTURING	5.875
	O-O	2.5	ADVANCED MEMORY SYSTEMS	8.000
3H	S-S	29.9	AIR REDUCTION	3.875
	A-A	31.8	ALASKA AIRLINES	6.500
5H	A-A	1.8	ALASKA AIRLINES	6.875
	S-S	7.8	ALASKA INTERSTATE	6.000
	S-S	20.0	ALEXANDERS INC	5.500

Indicated Common Div'd

The fourth column from the extreme right, this gives the annual dividend paid out to the common stock in the most recent twelve-month period, and becomes an important part of the computer calculations which we shall soon be dealing with.

Notes

This last column in the "permanent" programming, refers the subscriber to the R.H.M. Convertible Survey to the last page of the text portion of each week's Survey, where numbered "Notes" spell out any unique characteristics of the specific Convertible. Thus, some Bonds and Preferred Stocks are convertible into the common stocks of *another* company, often arising in a merger or acquisition, or in some other way. For example, the Apache Corp. 6s of 1990 are convertible, *not* into the common stock of Apache Corp., but into the common stock of *Continental Telephone*

Mat.	CONVERSION		Yr. Conv. Exp.	PRICE		Common Conv. Value	Prem. C/V (%)
	Price ($)	Rate (Shares)		Com.	Bond.		

CONVERTIBLE BONDS

Mat.	Price ($)	Rate (Shares)			Yr. Conv. Exp.	Com.	Bond.	Common Conv. Value	Prem. C/V (%)
81	57.11	1.751	TO	MAT	81	21.8	84.0	38.2	120
88	13.55	7.380	TO	MAT	88	16.6	121.0	122.5	0
96	101.33	.987	TO	MAT	96	56.5	73.1	55.8	31
87	58.50	1.709	TO	MAT	87	9.5	56.0	16.2	246
88	12.97	7.710	TO	MAT	88	7.0	62.5	54.0	16
91	8.82	11.338	TO	MAT	91	8.3	94.5	94.1	0
87	31.25	3.200	TO	MAT	87	22.9	84.0	73.3	15
86	6.62	15.106	TO	MAT	86	5.5	93.0	83.1	12
87	7.52	13.299	TO	MAT	87	5.5	82.0	73.1	12
96	26.00	3.846	TO	MAT	96	15.1	78.8	58.1	36
96	32.25	3.100	TO	MAT	96	8.0	58.5	24.8	136

ESL	INDICATED COMMON		Cur. Bond Yield	Notes (Last Page)
	Div'd	Yield		
	1.24	5.7	5.1	
	1.00	6.0	4.8	
49	1.06	1.9	6.3	
	.24	2.5	7.8	
	.40	5.7	9.4	2
	.00	.0	8.5	
48	1.00	4.4	4.6	23
	.00	.0	7.0	
	.00	.0	8.4	
	.15	1.0	7.6	
	.10	1.3	9.4	

Company. The designation "83" in the "Notes" column alerts the subscriber to this fact, and turning to the appropriate page, he looks down to "83" and gets the proper information. Such "Notes" will also tell one when interest on

Group Rating	Tdd Com·Bd.	Outst'g (Mill $)	ISSUE	Rate (%)
	S-S	29.2	AMF INC	4.250
3H	S-S	8.8	APL CORP	5.750
4	S-S	40.0	ARA SERVICES INC	4.625
	S-S	25.0	A-T-O INC	4.375
	A-O	2.9	ABERDEEN MANUFACTURING	5.875
	O-O	2.5	ADVANCED MEMORY SYSTEMS	8.000
3H	S-S	29.9	AIR REDUCTION	3.875
	A-A	31.8	ALASKA AIRLINES	6.500
5H	A-A	1.8	ALASKA AIRLINES	6.875
	S-S	7.8	ALASKA INTERSTATE	6.000
	S-S	20.0	ALEXANDERS INC	5.500

a particular Convertible is not being paid, when interest might be payable in Canadian funds, and other specific attributes of the particular Convertible.

The "Heart" Of The Computer Program

Each week, the staff of the R.H.M. Convertible Survey takes the current price of each common stock and the current price of each Convertible Bond and Convertible Preferred Stock and feeds those prices into the computer program with its permanent features as noted above. Here is what emerges, and all the later chapters of this book will depend heavily upon exactly such information. The prices themselves are noted, of course, in the two columns under "Price," headed "Com." and "Bond" for the Convertible Bond segment, and "Com." and "Pfd." for the Convertible Preferred Stocks.

Mat.	CONVERSION Price ($)	CONVERSION Rate (Shares)			Yr. Conv. Exp.	PRICE Com.	PRICE Bond.	Common Conv. Value	Prem. C/V (%)

CONVERTIBLE BONDS

81	57.11	1.751	TO	MAT	81	21.8	84.0	38.2	120
88	13.55	7.380	TO	MAT	88	16.6	121.0	122.5	0
96	101.33	.987	TO	MAT	96	56.5	73.1	55.8	31
87	58.50	1.709	TO	MAT	87	9.5	56.0	16.2	246
88	12.97	7.710	TC	MAT	88	7.0	62.5	54.0	16
91	8.82	11.338	TO	MAT	91	8.3	94.5	94.1	0
87	31.25	3.200	TC	MAT	87	22.9	84.0	73.3	15
86	6.62	15.106	TO	MAT	86	5.5	93.0	83.1	12
87	7.52	13.299	TO	MAT	87	5.5	82.0	73.1	12
96	26.00	3.846	TO	MAT	96	15.1	78.8	58.1	36
96	32.25	3.100	TO	MAT	96	8.0	58.5	24.8	136

ESL	INDICATED COMMON Div'd	INDICATED COMMON Yield	Cur. Bond Yield	Notes (Last Page)
	1.24	5.7	5.1	
	1.00	6.0	4.8	
49	1.06	1.9	6.3	
	.24	2.5	7.8	
	.40	5.7	9.4	2
	.00	.0	8.5	
48	1.00	4.4	4.6	23
	.00	.0	7.0	
	.00	.0	8.4	
	.15	1.0	7.6	
	.10	1.3	9.4	

Common Conv. Value

Immediately after the columns giving us the current prices of common and Convertible is the column headed

Group Rating	Tdd Com-Bd.	Outst'g (Mill $)	ISSUE	Rate (%)
	S-S	29.2	AMF INC	4.250
3H	S-S	8.8	APL CORP	5.750
4	S-S	40.0	ARA SERVICES INC	4.625
	S-S	25.0	A-T-O INC	4.375
	A-O	2.9	ABERDEEN MANUFACTURING	5.875
	O-O	2.5	ADVANCED MEMORY SYSTEMS	8.000
3H	S-S	29.9	AIR REDUCTION	3.875
	A-A	31.8	ALASKA AIRLINES	6.500
5H	A-A	1.8	ALASKA AIRLINES	6.875
	S-S	7.8	ALASKA INTERSTATE	6.000
	S-S	20.0	ALEXANDERS INC	5.500

"Common Conv. Value" in which the computer takes each common stock price and multiplies it by the Conversion "Rate," which spells out the number of shares of common stock into which each $100 face value of Convertible Bond, or each share of Convertible Preferred Stock, is convertible.

Thus, the first Convertible Bond in our listings as we write is the AMF Inc. 4¼s of 1981. In the February 20, 1976 Survey the common stock is given as 21.8, which is actually 21¾, the needs of the computer requiring rounding out to the nearest decimal. Each $100 face value of Convertible Bond is convertible into 1.751 shares, so the computer multiplies 21.8 by 1.751 to give us a Conversion Value of 38.2.

Prem. C/V (%)

In the next column, headed as above, the computer calculates the *premium over Conversion Value* at which the Bond is actually selling. Thus, the Bond is selling at 84.0,

Mat.	CONVERSION Price ($)	Rate (Shares)	Yr. Conv. Exp.	PRICE Com.	Bond.	Common Conv. Value	Prem. C/V (%)
81	57.11	1.751 TO MAT	81	21.8	84.0	38.2	120
88	13.55	7.380 TO MAT	88	16.6	121.0	122.5	0
96	101.33	.987 TO MAT	96	56.5	73.1	55.8	31
87	58.50	1.709 TO MAT	87	9.5	56.0	16.2	246
88	12.97	7.710 TO MAT	88	7.0	62.5	54.0	16
91	8.82	11.338 TO MAT	91	8.3	94.5	94.1	0
87	31.25	3.200 TO MAT	87	22.9	84.0	73.3	15
86	6.62	15.106 TO MAT	86	5.5	93.0	83.1	12
87	7.52	13.299 TO MAT	87	5.5	82.0	73.1	12
96	26.00	3.846 TO MAT	96	15.1	78.8	58.1	36
96	32.25	3.100 TO MAT	96	8.0	58.5	24.8	136

CONVERTIBLE BONDS

ESL	INDICATED COMMON Div'd	Yield	Cur. Bond Yield	Notes (Last Page)
	1.24	5.7	5.1	
	1.00	6.0	4.8	
49	1.06	1.9	6.3	
	.24	2.5	7.8	
	.40	5.7	9.4	2
	.00	.0	8.5	
48	1.00	4.4	4.6	23
	.00	.0	7.0	
	.00	.0	8.4	
	.15	1.0	7.6	
	.10	1.3	9.4	

as noted in the Bond price column, and the computer determines that the price of 84.0 is 120% above the Conversion Value of 38.2. The Convertible Bond is selling *far*

Group Rating	Tdd Com·Bd.	Outst'g (Mill $)	ISSUE	Rate (%)
	S-S	29.2	AMF INC	4.250
3H	S-S	8.8	APL CORP	5.750
4	S-S	40.0	ARA SERVICES INC	4.625
	S-S	25.0	A-T-O INC	4.375
	A-O	2.9	ABERDEEN MANUFACTURING	5.875
	O-O	2.5	ADVANCED MEMORY SYSTEMS	8.000
3H	S-S	29.9	AIR REDUCTION	3.875
	A-A	31.8	ALASKA AIRLINES	6.500
5H	A-A	1.8	ALASKA AIRLINES	6.875
	S-S	7.8	ALASKA INTERSTATE	6.000
	S-S	20.0	ALEXANDERS INC	5.500

above its actual Conversion Value so that even with a sub-stantial percentage move in AMF common, it is obvious that nothing too much will be happening to the AMF Convertible 4¼s of 1981 on any immediate basis. This does *not* mean that this Convertible should be totally ignored, as in later chapters we will be discussing the investment potential of exactly such Convertibles selling considerably above their Conversion Value. But Convertibles with *small* premiums over Conversion Value have many more avenues of potential profit, and this makes the "Premium Over Conversion Value" of great importance.

Indicated Common Yield

The common dividend paid in the last twelve months now does its work as part of the permanent computer program, by allowing the computer to divide the common dividend by the current price of the common stock. In the case of AMF this involves dividing $1.24 by 21.8, giving us an

CONVERTIBLE BONDS

Mat.	CONVERSION Price ($)	CONVERSION Rate (Shares)	Yr. Conv. Exp.	PRICE Com.	PRICE Bond.	Common Conv. Value	Prem. C/V (%)	ESL	INDICATED COMMON Div'd	INDICATED COMMON Yield	Cur. Bond Yield	Notes (Last Page)
81	57.11	1.751 TO MAT	81	21.8	84.0	38.2	120		1.24	5.7	5.1	
88	13.55	7.380 TO MAT	88	16.6	121.0	122.5	0		1.00	6.0	4.8	
96	101.33	.987 TO MAT	96	56.5	73.1	55.8	31	49	1.06	1.9	6.3	
87	58.50	1.709 TO MAT	87	9.5	56.0	16.2	246		.24	2.5	7.8	
88	12.97	7.710 TC MAT	88	7.0	62.5	54.0	16		.40	5.7	9.4	2
91	8.82	11.338 TO MAT	91	8.3	94.5	94.1	0		.00	.0	8.5	
87	31.25	3.200 TC MAT	87	22.9	84.0	73.3	15	48	1.00	4.4	4.6	23
86	6.62	15.106 TO MAT	86	5.5	93.0	83.1	12		.00	.0	7.0	
87	7.52	13.299 TO MAT	87	5.5	82.0	73.1	12		.00	.0	8.4	
96	26.00	3.846 TO MAT	96	15.1	78.8	58.1	36		.15	1.0	7.6	
96	32.25	3.100 TO MAT	96	8.0	58.5	24.8	136		.10	1.3	9.4	

indicated common dividend yield of 5.7% (rounded to the last decimal).

Group Rating	Tdd Com-Bd.	Outst'g (Mill $)	ISSUE	Rate (%)
	S-S	29.2	AMF INC	4.250
3H	S-S	8.8	APL CORP	5.750
4	S-S	40.0	ARA SERVICES INC	4.625
	S-S	25.0	A-T-O INC	4.375
	A-O	2.9	ABERDEEN MANUFACTURING	5.875
	O-O	2.5	ADVANCED MEMORY SYSTEMS	8.000
3H	S-S	29.9	AIR REDUCTION	3.875
	A-A	31.8	ALASKA AIRLINES	6.500
5H	A-A	1.8	ALASKA AIRLINES	6.875
	S-S	7.8	ALASKA INTERSTATE	6.000
	S-S	20.0	ALEXANDERS INC	5.500

Current Bond Yield

The annual interest paid for each Convertible Bond is given in the "Rate" column, while the annual dividend paid on each Convertible Preferred Stock is given in the "Dividend" column in that section. When either of these figures is divided by the current price of the Convertible Bond or the Convertible Preferred Stock, the computer gives us the *Current Yield* on each. In the case of AMF 4¼s of 1981, the $4.25 interest on the Bond is divided by the current market price of the Bond at 84.0 to give us a Bond Yield of 5.1% (again rounded to the last decimal).

Mat.	CONVERSION Price ($)	Rate (Shares)	Yr. Conv. Exp.	PRICE Com.	Bond.	Common Conv. Value	Prem. C/V (%)

CONVERTIBLE BONDS

Mat.	Price ($)	Rate (Shares)	Yr. Conv. Exp.	Com.	Bond.	Common Conv. Value	Prem. C/V (%)
81	57.11	1.751 TO MAT	81	21.8	84.0	38.2	120
88	13.55	7.380 TO MAT	88	16.6	121.0	122.5	0
96	101.33	.987 TO MAT	96	56.5	73.1	55.8	31
87	58.50	1.709 TO MAT	87	9.5	56.0	16.2	246
88	12.97	7.710 TO MAT	88	7.0	62.5	54.0	16
91	8.82	11.338 TO MAT	91	8.3	94.5	94.1	0
87	31.25	3.200 TO MAT	87	22.9	84.0	73.3	15
86	6.62	15.106 TO MAT	86	5.5	93.0	83.1	12
87	7.52	13.299 TO MAT	87	5.5	82.0	73.1	12
96	26.00	3.846 TO MAT	96	15.1	78.8	58.1	36
96	32.25	3.100 TO MAT	96	8.0	58.5	24.8	136

ESL	INDICATED COMMON Div'd	Yield	Cur. Bond Yield	Notes (Last Page)
	1.24	5.7	5.1	
	1.00	6.0	4.8	
49	1.06	1.9	6.3	
	.24	2.5	7.8	
	.40	5.7	9.4	2
	.00	.0	8.5	
48	1.00	4.4	4.6	23
	.00	.0	7.0	
	.00	.0	8.4	
	.15	1.0	7.6	
	.10	1.3	9.4	

55

The Indispensable Aid Of The
Computerized Statistical Approach

When there were only 150 to 200 Convertibles in the late-1940's, at the outset of this writer's growing interest in "Opportunities In Convertibles," it was possible to keep track of them with the help, perhaps, of but one assistant using the ponderous electric calculator typical of that period. By the time the R.H.M. Convertible Survey began its work in 1956, with several hundred additional Convertibles already trading, it took more than 5 such electric calculators going all day long, to give us the information we have just described.

Today, with about *1,000* actively traded Convertible Bonds and Convertible Preferred Stocks, and so many additional profit techniques which we shall soon be describing such as the "Convertible Hedge" and the "Convertible/Call Option Hedge," the help of the computer becomes not only invaluable, but indispensable. The many avenues to stock market profits via the well-situated Convertible opened up by such computer analysis will become much clearer as the later chapters come into view.

The Immediate Uses Of The Computerized
Statistical Presentation Of 1,000 Convertibles

In our opening paragraphs we described how investors buying Pan American World Airways common stock at 4 in April 1975 were, through ignorance of the existence of a Pan American World Airways *Convertible Bond* selling at Conversion Parity and yielding 13.1%, throwing that 13.1% out the window to no purpose whatever. In the text which followed we demonstrated over and over again how a

Convertible selling at Conversion Parity *must* show just as much profit per dollar invested as the common stock on any *upside* move, *cannot* show any greater loss than the common per dollar invested on any *downside* move in the common, and most often would show less loss than the common on the downside, typically *far* less loss. With the Convertible scoring ahead of the common on every count, why buy the common instead of the Convertible and lose that 13.1% yield, in addition to all the other superior attributes of the Convertible?

We are certain the reader is completely convinced that there was *no* reason for an investor to buy Pan American common under those circumstances, and that he should have emphatically been buying the Pan American World Airways 7½s of 1998. *If* that investor had at hand the R.H.M. Convertible Survey of April 11, 1975 and had checked to see whether there was a Convertible trading for Pan American, he would have found not one, but *five* Convertible Bonds trading!

Group Rating	Tdd Com·Bd.	Outst'g (Mill $)	ISSUE	Rate (%)	Mat.	Price ($)
	A-A	6.1	OZARK AIR LINES	5.250	86	7.7
	A-A	15.0	OZARK AIR LINES	6.750	88	8.6
	O-O	2.0	PAN AMERICAN BANCSHARES	6.500	91	18.0
	S-S	4.1	PAN AMERICAN WORLD AIRWAYS	4.875	79	7.5
	S-S	24.9	PAN AMERICAN WORLD AIRWAYS	4.500	84	12.9
	S-S	175.0	PAN AMERICAN WORLD AIRWAYS	5.250	89	24.1
	S-S	175.0	PAN AMERICAN WORLD AIRWAYS	4.500	86	29.3
3	S-S	75.0	PAN AMERICAN WORLD AIRWAYS	7.500	98	7.0
	S-S	15.0	PAPERCRAFT CORP	5.250	94	31.9
3H	S-S	20.0	PARKER-HANNIFIN CORP	4.000	92	50.6
	S-S	23.5	PENN-DIXIE INDUSTRIES INC	5.000	82	20.3
3	S-S	50.0	PENNSYLVANIA CO	9.000	94	81.9
	C-C	9.3	PENNSYLVANIA ENGINEERING	5.000	93	9.7
4	S-S	50.0	PENNZOIL CO	5.250	96	38.2
	O-O	130.0	PENNZOIL LA & TEX OFFSHORE	1.000	79	6.2
	S-S	50.0	PEPSICO	4.750	96	63.5
	S-O	3.5	PEPSI-COLA GEN BOTTLERS	5.500	88	66.2
	A-A	7.7	PERMANEER CORP	5.250	89	29.2
	A-A	5.1	PERMANEER CORP	7.000	91	13.0
	O-O	15.0	PETTIBONE MULLIKEN CORP	4.625	87	33.3
	S-S	100.0	PFIZER INC	4.000	97	47.5
	S-S	10.0	PHILLIPS-VAN HEUSEN CORP	5.250	94	28.1
4H 3	A-A	9.9	PHOENIX STEEL CORP	6.000	87	11.5
	O-O	7.0	PIEDMONT AVIATION	5.375	86	14.9

Looking at the excerpt from the computerized statistical tables in the Survey of April 11, 1975 we note first the premiums over Conversion Value ("Prem C/V %") for each of the five Convertible Bonds. The 7½s of 1998 were the closest to 0 premium—a 2% premium being, for all practical purposes, a 0 premium, and the Convertible having sold at an exact 0 premium on different occasions in that week. The tables would immediately have shown a prospective buyer of Pan American common that he should, *instead,* be buying the Convertible 7½s of 1998.

Nor were the other four Convertible Bonds of Pan American devoid of interest. As we move along, readers will take note of the obvious fact that all the advantages we are detailing for well-situated Convertibles do *not* rely upon a

SION Rate (Shares)	Yr. Conv. Exp.	PRICE Com.	PRICE Bond.	Common Conv. Value	Prem. C/V (%)	ESL	INDICATED COMMON Div'd	INDICATED COMMON Yield	Cur. Bond Yield	Notes (Last Page)
,903 TO MAT	86	3.0	56.0	38.7	45		.05	1.7	9.4	
,553 TO.MAT	88	3.0	59.5	34.7	72		.05	1.7	11.3	
,555 TO MAT	91	6.1	61.0	33.9	80		.54	8.9	10.7	
,333 TO MAT	79	4.0	72.0	53.3	35		.00	.0	6.8	
,716 TO MAT	84	4.0	42.6	30.9	38		.00	.0	10.6	
,136 TO MAT	89	4.0	28.8	16.5	75		.00	.0	18.2	
,405 TO MAT	86	4.0	27.0	13.6	99		.00	.0	16.7	
,286 TO MAT	98	4.0	58.1	57.1	2		.00	.0	12.9	
,133 TO MAT	94	7.8	57.0	24.4	134		.60	7.7	9.2	2
,974 TO MAT	92	16.6	52.0	32.8	59		1.12	6.7	7.7	
,921 TO MAT	82	6.1	72.1	30.0	140		.24	3.9	6.9	
,219 TO 4-79	79	65.1	91.5	79.4	15		5.00	7.7	9.8	29
,256 TO MAT	93	1.8	38.0	18.5	105		.05	2.8	13.2	
,614 TO MAT	96	17.3	64.0	45.2	42		1.20	6.9	8.2	
,000 TO MAT	79	3.0	74.0	48.0	54		.00	.0	1.4	37
,575 TO MAT	96	57.0	100.8	89.8	12	56	1.40	2.5	4.7	
,509 TO MAT	88	34.0	55.0	51.3	7		3.50	10.3	10.0	78
,423 TO MAT	89	1.9	23.8	6.5	266		.00	.0	22.1	
,692 TO MAT	91	1.9	32.0	14.6	119		.00	.0	21.9	
,000 TO MAT	87	17.3	66.5	51.9	28		.60	3.5	7.0	75
,105 TO MAT	97	32.0	89.5	67.4	33	50	.76	2.4	4.5	
,556 TO MAT	89	5.5	55.5	19.6	183		.40	7.3	9.5	
,666 TO MAT	87	6.4	69.0	55.5	24		.00	.0	8.7	
,689 TO MAT	86	5.1	58.0	34.1	70		.40	7.8	9.3	

Convertible selling at *exact* Conversion Parity, at 0 premium. This narrow and unnecessary course would mean that we would be ignoring hundreds of superb opportunities, for premiums over Conversion Value of 5%, 10% and even higher for various purposes, still allow superior benefits, the premiums merely diminishing to a typically minor degree, the yield and profit potential, and representing, in effect, an insurance payment we are making for those benefits. In most cases, a small premium over Conversion Value is certainly desirable, and we look for them assiduously. But by no means do we ignore Convertible opportunities along the lines we have described, and will be describing, because a modest premium over Conversion Value exists.

In the excerpt from the R.H.M. Convertible Survey of

Group Rating	Tdd Com-Bd.	Outst'g (Mill $)	ISSUE	Rate (%)	Mat.	Price ($)
	A-A	6.1	OZARK AIR LINES	5.250	86	7.75
	A-A	15.0	OZARK AIR LINES	6.750	88	8.66
	0-0	2.0	PAN AMERICAN BANCSHARES	6.500	91	18.00
	S-S	4.1	PAN AMERICAN WORLD AIRWAYS	4.875	79	7.50
	S-S	24.9	PAN AMERICAN WORLD AIRWAYS	4.500	84	12.96
	S-S	175.0	PAN AMERICAN WORLD AIRWAYS	5.250	89	24.18
	S-S	175.0	PAN AMERICAN WORLD AIRWAYS	4.500	86	29.3
3	S-S	75.0	PAN AMERICAN WORLD AIRWAYS	7.500	98	7.00
	S-S	15.0	PAPERCRAFT CORP	5.250	94	31.9
3H	S-S	20.0	PARKER-HANNIFIN CORP	4.000	92	50.6
	S-S	23.5	PENN-DIXIE INDUSTRIES INC	5.000	82	20.3
3	S-S	50.0	PENNSYLVANIA CO	9.000	94	81.9
	C-C	9.3	PENNSYLVANIA ENGINEERING	5.000	93	9.75
4	S-S	50.0	PENNZOIL CO	5.250	96	38.2
	0-0	130.0	PENNZOIL LA & TEX OFFSHORE	1.000	79	6.2
	S-S	50.0	PEPSICO	4.750	96	63.5
	S-0	3.5	PEPSI-COLA GEN BOTTLERS	5.500	88	66.2
	A-A	7.7	PERMANEER CORP	5.250	89	29.2
	A-A	5.1	PERMANEER CORP	7.000	91	13.0
	0-0	15.0	PETTIBONE MULLIKEN CORP	4.625	87	33.3
	S-S	100.0	PFIZER INC	4.000	97	47.5
	S-S	10.0	PHILLIPS-VAN HEUSEN CORP	5.250	94	28.1
4H 3	A-A	9.9	PHOENIX STEEL CORP	6.000	87	11.5
	0-0	7.0	PIEDMONT AVIATION	5.375	86	14.9

April 11, 1975 shown, for example, an investor mostly interested in *yield,* might find the Pan American 5¼s of 1989 to his liking because of the *18.2% yield.* Did the very large 75% premium completely divorce such a purchase from possible eventual upside capital appreciation? Not at all, since with each $100 face value of the 5¼s of 1998 convertible into 4.136 shares of Pan American common, the later rise of that common stock to a price of, say, 10, would give the Convertible a minimum market value of 10 x 4.136 or 41⅜ which would still represent a 43% advance over the 28⅞ (28.8) price shown for that Convertible Bond in April 1975.

RSION Rate (Shares)			Yr. Conv. Exp.	PRICE		Common Conv. Value	Prem. C/V (%)	ESL	INDICATED COMMON		Cur. Bond Yield	Notes (Last Page)
				Com.	Bond.				Div'd	Yield		
.903	TO	MAT	86	3.0	56.0	38.7	45		.05	1.7	9.4	
.553	TO	MAT	88	3.0	59.5	34.7	72		.05	1.7	11.3	
.555	TO	MAT	91	6.1	61.0	33.9	80		.54	8.9	10.7	
.333	TO	MAT	79	4.0	72.0	53.3	35		.00	.0	6.8	
.716	TO	MAT	84	4.0	42.6	30.9	38		.00	.0	10.6	
.136	TO	MAT	89	4.0	28.8	16.5	75		.00	.0	18.2	
.405	TO	MAT	86	4.0	27.0	13.6	99		.00	.0	16.7	
.286	TO	MAT	98	4.0	58.1	57.1	2		.00	.0	12.9	
.133	TO	MAT	94	7.8	57.0	24.4	134		.60	7.7	9.2	2
.974	TO	MAT	92	16.6	52.0	32.8	59		1.12	6.7	7.7	
.921	TO	MAT	82	6.1	72.1	30.0	140		.24	3.9	6.9	
.219	TO	4-79	79	65.1	91.5	79.4	15		5.00	7.7	9.8	29
.256	TO	MAT	93	1.8	38.0	18.5	105		.05	2.8	13.2	
.614	TO	MAT	96	17.3	64.0	45.2	42		1.20	6.9	8.2	
.000	TO	MAT	79	3.0	74.0	48.0	54		.00	.0	1.4	37
.575	TO	MAT	96	57.0	100.8	89.8	12	56	1.40	2.5	4.7	
.509	TO	MAT	88	34.0	55.0	51.3	7		3.50	10.3	10.0	78
.423	TO	MAT	89	1.9	23.8	6.5	266		.00	.0	22.1	
.692	TO	MAT	91	1.9	32.0	14.6	119		.00	.0	21.9	
.105	TO	MAT	97	32.0	89.5	67.4	33	50	.76	2.4	4.5	
.556	TO	MAT	89	5.5	55.5	19.6	183		.40	7.3	9.5	
.666	TO	MAT	87	6.4	69.0	55.5	24		.00	.0	8.7	
.689	TO	MAT	86	5.1	58.0	34.1	70		.40	7.8	9.3	

The virtually 0 premium for the 7½s of 1998 made that Convertible the vehicle of choice, of course, but there are a *number* of Convertible strategies which utilize relatively high-premium Convertibles for quite worthwhile yield and profit objectives and we shall be discussing them in later chapters.

More Examples From The Statistical Tables

The function of the computerized statistical approach is so central to all Convertible strategy that we should carefully study some additional examples.

From the R.H.M. Convertible Survey of February 20, 1976, we take one excerpt from the Convertible Bond section, and one from the Convertible Preferred Stock section. Note the low premium over Conversion Value in the Convertible Bond segment for the Jim Walter 5¾s of 1991 with the superior yield of the Bond as against the common stock.

Group Rating	Tdd Com-Bd.	Outst'g (Mill $)	ISSUE	Rate (%)	Mat.	CON Price ($)
	S-S	10.5	ITEL CORP	7.000	95	18.50
	S-S	20.0	ITEL CORP	8.000	96	15.00
	A-O	2.0	JETRONIC INDUSTRIES	6.250	88	10.50
3H	S-S	35.0	JIM WALTER	5.750	91	42.00
	S-O	7.0	JOSTENS INC	4.750	88	36.36
3H	O-O	3.7	KAMAN CORP	4.750	87	26.36
	O-O	4.3	KEYES FIBRE	5.250	85	25.00
	O-O	6.0	KEYES FIBRE	5.000	92	26.00
	S-O	10.7	KEYSTONE STEEL & WIRE	4.500	81	40.00
	S-S	9.8	KIRSCH COMPANY	6.000	95	32.44
	S-S	200.0	KRESGE S S	6.000	99	35.50
	S-S	36.4	LTV CORP	7.500	77	10.50

Group Rating	Tdd Com-Pfd.	Outst'g (000 Shs.)	ISSUE	Div.	Par	CON Price ($)
	S-S	257.0	COOPER INDUSTRIES B	2.500	NP	0
	S-S	300.0	COOPER TIRE & RUBBER	1.250	25	27.00
3	S-S	914.0	CROCKER NATIONAL	3.000	NP	0
3	S-S	468.2	CROUSE-HINDS	3.350	NP	0
	O-O	320.0	CRUM & FORSTER A	2.400	5	31.25
	S-S	250.0	CUMMINS ENGINE CO	7.500	NP	37.00
	S-S	249.0	CURTISS-WRIGHT CORP A	2.000	1	32.00
	C-O	1823.3	DWG CORP	.350	1	0
3	S-S	2980.0	DART INDUSTRIES	2.000	5	0
	S-S	75.0	DAYCO CORP A	4.250	NP	0
3	S-S	492.0	DENNISON MANUFACTURING CO	1.000	10	0
	S-O	402.0	DENNYS INC	1.000	NP	0

Note also the 0 premium for Kaman Corp. 4¾s of 1987, the 0 premium for Keyes Fibre 5s of 1992 and the near-0 premium over Conversion Value of 2% for LTV 7½s of 1977.

Turning to the Convertible Preferred Stock section, we note the small 5% premium for the Crouse-Hinds $3.35 Preferred Stock, the 0 premium for the DWG Corp. $0.35 Preferred Stock and the negligible 2% premium for Dayco Corp. A $4.25 Preferred Stock.

RSION Rate (Shares)			Yr. Conv. Exp.	PRICE Com.	Bond.	Common Conv. Value	Prem. C/V (%)	Inv. Val.	INDICATED COMMON Div'd	Yield	Cur. Bond Yield	Notes (Last Page)
.405	TC	MAT	95	8.9	74.0	48.1	54		.20	2.2	9.5	
.666	TO	MAT	96	8.9	84.0	59.3	42		.20	2.2	9.5	
.524	TO	12-76	88	4.4	52.5	41.9	25		.00	.0	11.9	
.380	TO	MAT	91	43.6	110.0	103.8	6		1.00	2.3	5.2	
.750	TO	MAT	88	21.8	76.0	60.0	27	58	1.00	4.6	6.3	
.794	TO	MAT	87	22.4	85.0	85.0	0		.80	3.6	5.6	
.000	TO	MAT	85	18.8	79.0	75.2	5		1.00	5.3	6.6	
.846	TO	MAT	92	18.8	72.3	72.3	0		1.00	5.3	6.9	
.500	TO	MAT	81	19.8	79.5	49.5	61		1.00	5.1	5.7	51
.C83	TO	MAT	95	15.8	77.0	48.7	58	58	.90	5.7	7.8	
.817	TO	MAT	99	33.0	111.5	93.0	20	64	.24	.7	5.4	
.524	TO	MAT	77	12.9	125.0	122.9	2		.00	.0	6.0	

RSION Rate (Shares)	Yr. Conv. Exp.	PRICE Com.	Pfd.	Common Conv. Value	Prem. C/V (%)	INDICATED COMMON Div'd	Yield	Cur. Pf'd Yield	Notes (Last Page)
1.800		57.5	102.0	103.5	0	1.68	2.9	2.5	
.926		14.0	16.0	13.0	23	.60	4.3	7.8	
1.500		24.8	41.5	37.2	12	1.66	6.7	7.2	
2.440		22.6	58.0	55.1	5	.80	3.5	5.8	2
3.200		26.1	84.0	83.5	1	1.40	5.4	2.9	
2.703		25.0	91.5	67.6	35	1.00	4.0	8.2	
1.250		14.4	25.5	18.0	42	.40	2.8	7.8	7
1.210		3.8	4.6	4.6	0	.00	.0	7.6	1
1.000		34.6	37.8	34.6	9	.64	1.8	5.3	2
3.750		15.1	57.5	56.6	2	.50	3.3	7.4	
.750		28.3	20.5	21.2	0	1.00	3.5	4.9	
2.500		21.6	55.3	Called at 33.50 on 4-9-76					

The Computerized Statistical Tables—
Our Constant Companions!

The ceaselessly changing tides in the stock market, with thousands of common stocks climbing to the upside, slipping to the downside, different Groups of stocks coming to the fore or fading away, individual stocks getting ready to make financial headlines—*all* of these movements are mirrored in the Convertible tables when there is a Convertible Bond or a Convertible Preferred Stock trading along with those common stocks. And it should be crystal clear by this point that *no* move should ever be taken with a common stock without first consulting the Convertible tables to determine whether there *is* an applicable Convertible, and whether its statistical position is such that it presents an alternative to the common stock.

When the answer is "yes" to the two questions just stated, the advantages of the Convertible can be so large that *not* having checked before purchasing any common stock could very easily turn into a major financial blunder, not only losing money in accepting lower yields and higher commission rates, but in exposing one's capital to totally unnecessary greater risk of loss.

Beyond these first factors of the potentially superior characteristics of the well-situated Convertible, there are many other profit avenues inherent in the Convertible itself which we have not yet touched upon. But before we begin that important part of this inquiry into "Stock Market Profits With Convertibles" let us more closely examine an important element in understanding Convertibles, which we have touched on only slightly up to this point.

The publisher, R.H.M. Press, has agreed to make available to the reader, at no extra charge, a Special Supplement, giving the author's current and completely updated analysis and statistical presentation of the entire list of currently outstanding Convertible Bonds and Convertible Preferred Stocks, including a statistical presentation of Euro-Convertible Bonds and Convertibles with Call Option Hedge Potential, in accordance with the description of these areas of "Opportunities In Convertibles" set forth in this book.

To receive this Special Supplement, important to following current opportunities, send your name and address—be sure to include zip—to:

R.H.M. Press Dept. 85
840 Willis Avenue
Albertson, Long Island
New York 11507

There will be no charge for this Special Supplement.

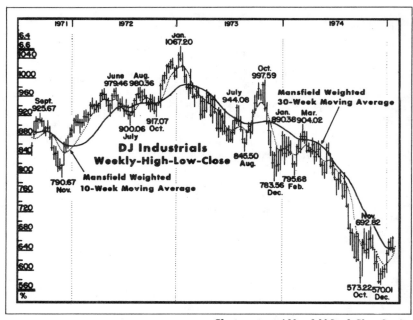

Chart courtesy of Mansfield Stock Chart Service

The MOST Important Contribution
Of the Convertible

Opposite is a chart of the Dow-Jones Industrial Average, courtesy of Mansfield Stock Chart Service, February 1975. A withering decline from the January 1973 high has devastated wide sections of the market and now, in early-1975, a modest upturn is taking place. Does this upturn mark the end of the entire 1973-1974 disaster, the prelude to a vigorous upturn which could produce large market profits in 1975? Or is this modest upturn a mere "intermediate recovery" such as took place in October 1973, in March 1974 and in November 1974, each time to be followed by sinking spells to new lows, piling new losses on top of old losses?

The fact is that in early-1975 nobody could know the answer to that question with certainty. One could have opinions, even strong opinions, and marshal logic and facts to support those opinions. But certainty in the stock market?— Never.

Shell-shocked by the ravages to their pocketbooks of what had already taken place 1973 through 1974, the vast majority of investors were unquestionably standing on the sidelines, afraid to enlarge commitments in early 1975 and, therefore, missing the dramatic upside leap which did in fact take place as shown by the same chart, from the same source which appeared 9 months later in December 1975.

67

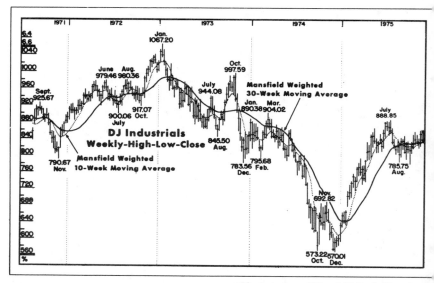

Chart courtesy of Mansfield Stock Chart Servic

Now, *had* these investors been fully conversant with the logic of the Convertible, and been aware of the various "Opportunities In Convertibles" which are present at almost any stage of any stock market cycle, they would have found it much more possible to set aside fear and timidity and to participate in that substantial market rally of the first half of 1975, and beyond to its continuation through early-1976.

Norton Simon $1.60 Convertible Preferred

Here, for example was Norton Simon $1.60 Convertible Preferred in the first week of January 1975 selling at 23⅞ with the common stock at 10⅜. The modest 10% premium over Conversion Value meant the Convertible would lag any upside move of the common by a trifling amount, but this slight diminution of advantage had to pale in light of the 6.7% yield on the Convertible Preferred as against the 3.9% yield on the common *and,* most importantly, that when Norton Simon common hit its 1974 low at 7¾, the Convertible Preferred did not sell down to *its* Conversion low at 16¼, but sold no lower than *19.*

Norton Simon Convertible Preferred was promising a higher yield and better downside protection than the common stock, and could have been purchased with much more confidence than the common stock because of these factors. When the common stock did indeed move from recovery to boom, moving from 10⅜ to 22⅞ by March 1976, the Norton Simon $1.60 Convertible Preferred moved right along with the common to the upside on its Conversion Value, advancing more than 100% from 23⅞ to 48½.

The Convertible Preferred had shown almost exactly the same percentage gain on the upside, *but* and it was an important "but," *could have been purchased with much more assurance* in January 1975 because of the heightened downside protection to capital—a vital factor in fear-ridden January 1975.

Jim Walter $1.60 Convertible Preferred

Along exactly the same line, in mid-December 1974, directly before the actual market turn commenced, when almost all investors were assuredly hiding under their respective beds, they should have been looking at Jim Walter $1.60 Convertible Preferred which was selling at 24 with the common at 20⅞. Each share of the $1.60 Preferred was convertible into 1.08 shares of common at any time and a minor 7% premium held sway. The same advantages were discernible, the yield on the Convertible being 6.7% against 3.8% for the common, and the 1974 low for common and Convertible revealing that the $1.60 Preferred of Jim Walter had held up markedly better in 1974 than the common stock, and would doubtless do so again if another market spill was in the offing.

Instead of a spill came the rise and Jim Walter common surged from 20⅞ to 41⅜ by March, 1976. The $1.60 Convertible Preferred matched that rise virtually dollar-for-dollar, moving from 24 to 45, another near-100% move.

And, to repeat the vital factor once again—an investor knowledgeable in Convertibles could, in December 1974, have acted with much more boldness with the protective features of the Convertible as against the unsheltered common stock.

Harman International Industries 5⅜s of 1982

One of the beauties of watching 1,000 Convertibles is the way *new* opportunities move into view in a virtually continuous stream during a pervasive market movement. Thus, as a market moves to swift recovery, a Convertible which may have been perched considerably above the common stock, selling at a high premium over conversion Value, becomes a timely commitment when a rapid upside run in the common stock quickly shrinks the premium to a minor dimension, allowing the Convertible to deck itself in all its superior garments of higher yield, better downside protection against loss, and lower commission costs.

Thus, in April 1975, with the market recovery already well along, Harman International Industries 5⅜s of 1982 could have been found in the Convertible statistical tables with its premium over Conversion Value shrunken to a mere 3%, and the Convertible yielding 6% against a miniscule 0.4% for the common stock. Checking back into how common and Convertible behaved at the early-1975 lows would have crowned the Convertible with the laurel wreath of "Greater Safety," the actual 61 low for the Convertible contrasting with the lowly 5⅛ figure for the common, at which price the straight Conversion Value of the Bond was only *35.81,* rather than its actual low of 61.

Certainly, with these figures, one could have been buying the Convertible Bond in April 1975 with *much* more assurance than the common stock, and getting a 6% yield to boot against that 0.4% yield for the common. When the common stock ran from 12½ to 26½, the Convertible Bond was matching it all the way, moving from 89½ to 205.

71

All Market Recoveries Show the Same Pattern
Of Convertible Superiority

Not only could many more examples be cited from the 1975 rise, but going back to previous recoveries from shattering market declines such as the 1969-1970 period and others *must* show the same pattern because of the very nature of the Convertible in so often providing a superior yield and better downside protection, the reasons for which favorable attributes we have discussed in previous chapters.

The major point to be appreciated with these superior features is that at market lows the investor familiar with Convertibles *is able to act more aggressively, with greater boldness,* and therefore benefits to a far greater extent than the very large number of investors who, carrying over the disheartening fears of the just-experienced market devastation, fail to move into a recovering market until its most highly-leveraged portion is already history.

All along the market rise, new Convertibles move into strategic positions, as described with the Harman International example, enabling participation in the further rise on a reduced-risk basis and, thereby, continuing the advantage of being able to act with greater boldness.

The stellar role played by well-situated Convertibles during the initial recovery phase and all through the subsequent rise must be given full weight by all thinking investors, if successful results are to be achieved.

The Equally Great Contribution At Market Tops

Following is another chart from Mansfield Stock Chart Service, this time from the bull market *top* of December

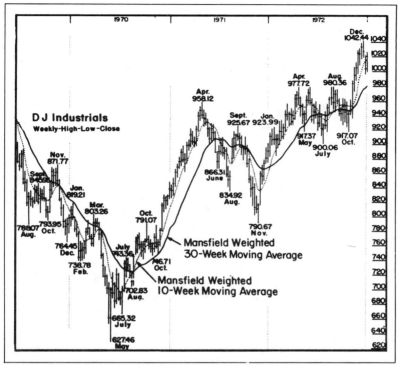

Chart courtesy of Mansfield Stock Chart Service

1972- - January 1973. Measured from the 1970 bottom, a rise of very large proportions had taken place. Was the advance to go still further, to new uncharted heights in the Dow-Jones Industrials of 1,200, even 1,500? Probably many investors thought so, examining the elevated price/earnings ratios at which so many stocks were selling. Indeed, it is typical of a bull market top that investors have the courage of lions, the opposite of the fear and timidity which beset them at market lows!

Obviously, the reverse should hold sway, one being eager to buy at low levels when true bargains are available from the point of view of assets and earnings, and reluctant to buy at market tops when most values are ridiculously overpriced. But it is an unquestioned fact that emotion rules at tops and at bottoms, causing buying to take place when one should be selling, and selling to take place when one should be buying.

Once again well-situated Convertibles are ready to step into the breach for those investors who are familiar with their favorable characteristics. Since one really does not know at any stage of the market cycle whether a market top *is* really at hand, or whether stocks will simply continue to march on to still higher, and still more overvalued levels, why not shift a greater part of one's investments *away* from the common stocks and *towards* well-situated Convertibles? The simple fact, as we have seen, is that if a market top does indeed eventuate, one's losses will be much smaller than if one continued holding the common stocks. And, on the other hand, if the market is truly going to move on to still higher levels, the Convertible will share virtually dollar-for-dollar invested in the further market profits, just as if one had continued to hold the riskier common stocks.

All this becomes very clear when we pick a spot near what proved to be the actual top of the rise, the prelude to market disaster, and see how a selection of Convertibles fared as against their common stocks. All the examples cited are from the week-ending November 24, 1972, quite near the January 1973 market top, and we then examine where Convertible and common stood in the week-ending August 31, 1973, when the first heavy blow of the 1973-

1974 bear market had already been experienced.

Belden Corp. 8s of 1990

In November 1972 the common stock was at 27½ and the Convertible Bond at 112½. There was only a 2% premium over Conversion Value for the Bond so any further rise in the common would have been exactly matched by the Convertible Bond, dollar-for-dollar invested. Further, the Convertible was yielding 7.1% and the common only 4.4%. (Why would anyone foolishly be holding the Convertible rather than the common given these figures? Well, the specific purpose of this book is to dissuade readers from *further* such foolishness, in current and future markets!)

Came the market crack and by August 1973, Belden common had dropped to 20¾, down 24.5%, while the Convertible Bond had also dropped from 112.50 to 100.00, but this was only an 11.1% decline. The Convertible Bond had shown considerably less than *half* the percentage loss suffered by the common.

Jostens Inc. 4¾s of 1988

In November 1972, this leading manufacturer of school class rings and yearbooks saw its common stock selling at 30½ with its Convertible 4¾s of 1988 selling at 84½. There was a modest 11% premium over Conversion Value for the Convertible Bond, and the Bond was yielding 5.6% against a 2.4% yield for the common stock. By August 1973, Jostens common had dropped from 30½ to 16⅝, down 45.5%, while the Convertible Bond had dropped from 84½ to 66½, down only 21.3%. Again, the Convertible Bond would have shown almost the same appreciation as the common stock if a further rise in the common had actually taken place, but endured less than ½ the actual percentage loss suffered by the common stock when a decline ensued rather than an advance.

Kirsch 6s of 1995

In November 1972 this top name in quality drapery saw its common stock selling at 35⅞ while its Convertible Bond, the 6s of 1995, was selling at 115.0, about 4% above actual Conversion Value. Came the 1973 market bust and by August 1973 the common stock was down to 16⅛ for a loss of 55.1%. For the same period of time, the Convertible Bond had dropped only from 115 to 85⅛, down 26.0%. Again, the common stock had shown a decline more than twice as great as for the Convertible.

Wayne Mfg. 4⅞s of 1987

The statistics remain quite uniform. In November 1972 the common stock was selling at 24¼ and the Convertible Bond at 82. The premium over Conversion Value was 5% so, for all practical purposes, each $1 invested in the Convertible Bond would show exactly as much percentage profit as the same $1 invested in the common stock. The Convertible Bond was yielding 5.9%, *4½ times* the 1.3% yield on the common stock and, yes, there is that extra salt for the wound of the common stock costing 3 times as much in commissions to buy as for the same dollar amount of the Convertible Bond. Remarkable, the self-injury of the investor who doesn't know how to follow, and use, Convertibles.

76

By August 1973 there was the familiar result. Wayne Mfg. common had dropped from 24¼ to 16½, down 32%. The Wayne Mfg. Convertible Bonds had, in exactly the same time period, dropped from 82 to 70½, down only *14%*. Again, the percentage loss in the common had been considerably more than twice as much as the percentage loss in the Convertible.

Occidental Petroleum $3.60 Preferred

One quick example from the Convertible Preferred segment. In November 1972, the common stock of Occidental Petroleum was selling at 13⅛, while its $3.60 Convertible Preferred Stock was selling at 46½, at a premium over Conversion Value of 11%. The Convertible was yielding 7.7%, the common was paying no dividend at all, and yielding 0. By August 1973, the common stock had declined from 13⅛ to 9, down 31.4%, while the Convertible Preferred had dropped from 46½ to 40½, down 12.9. The common stock had suffered almost 2½ times the loss in the Convertible.

The Great Flexibility Of The Well-Situated Convertible

Many more examples could have been cited, not only from the November 1972 - August 1973 period, but from any other market top we could have studied. Having followed Convertibles on a virtually daily basis for about thirty years, this writer could fill several books just with examples of what we have described above.

Now, the crucial point here is that a thorough knowledge of about 1,000 Convertibles, Convertible Bonds and Convertible Preferred Stocks, will *always* reveal a substantial number of strategically-poised Convertibles which allow for full, or nearly full, participation in any upside move of the common, but allow the holder to sidestep a large part of the losses if the common stock, instead of moving up, moves down. Even forgetting the very often far higher yields and lower commission costs obtainable through the respective Convertible, this equal reward/lower risk attribute of the well-situated Convertible leads the knowledgeable investor to a greater share of the leveraged profits available when a devastated market bottoms out and turns to the upside.

Of equal benefit, this same indisputable logic protects and enhances capital at market tops in two ways. First, one does not, after all, *know* that the market has reached its upper limit for that market move and is preparing to spill to the downside, until the hurtful event actually occurs. If one merely *believes* the market is topping out and retreats to the sidelines, and is proved wrong by events, then one has missed the heady and rapid additional market profits typical near excited highs. How much better *to shift funds from common stocks to a greater proportion of Convertibles,* "buying" downside insurance and yet leaving oneself free to share in any further upside profits.

Secondly, if it really does prove to be a market top and a slide commences, one's capital not only suffers far less in the Convertible than in the common stock, as we have described, but one hardly needs to wait until the common stock has dropped by 50%! Thus, the tenets of "Technical Analysis of Stocks" permit one to become aware that the market decline has become pervasive and that a market top has already been experienced when, say, about 25% damage has been done to the common stock. At such a point, the percentage damage to the Convertible is very often far less than what takes place when the common stock decline has reached the levels of 50% off the highs.

With such attention paid to technical indicators, the Convertible positions themselves can be adjusted well before the major part of the slide has taken place, either being sold out or, better still, converted to Full-Hedge positions to *benefit* from further declining markets. (We will shortly say something about the explanations of the "Convertible Hedge" to come in later chapters.)

What we have described above is also true near the termination of market *declines,* when one does not really know for certain that another round of losses is not coming up. Taking our Convertible positions permits participation in the upside profits *if* events actually demonstrate that a market bottom has truly arrived, and a sustained upswing begins. But if some market uplift proves temporary and a slide to new lows begins, one need not simply sit with Convertible positions when technical indicators again are informing us that a "lower low" is on the way. Once again, the Convertible positions can be liquidated or, again better still, the *Convertible Hedge* can be brought into play.

Thus, the very felicitous *flexibility* of the Convertible near market tops and market bottoms and, indeed, at any stage of the market cycle, always allowing the investor to deal on such a better level with his typically self-defeating emotional responses at such respective tops and bottoms when his instincts are always pushing him in the wrong direction!

79

This, then, is the most favorable aspect of the Convertible, allowing 1,000 Convertibles to work for heightened profit participation at any stage of market movement in a manner which the reader should not underestimate as to its actual scope. Standing aside from market opportunities near bottoms can lose some of the most rapid and leveraged gains of the market cycle. Knowledgeable use of Convertibles *allows* participation in those gains. And remaining hip-deep in overvalued common stocks can lead to horrendous losses when the sickening slide begins. Knowledgeable use of Convertible *prevents* much of those losses. We feel it would be difficult to overestimate the value of following Convertibles as completely as possible in the face of such important contributions to investment success.

The Convertible Hedge

Pausing for one additional small chapter which returns us to the important question of *why* Convertible senior securities hold up better than their respective common stocks in falling markets—it is vital for the reader to have a full comprehension of this central market phenomenon—we will then launch into a discussion of one of the most fascinating and potential-filled aspects of the Convertible—the Convertible Hedge. Not to leave the reader in complete suspense, the Convertible Hedge involves being simultanously *Long* the Convertible and *Short* the common in varying proportions to reach varying goals. Proper use of the Convertible Hedge takes all the favorable aspects of Convertibles which we have described thus far and elevates them to even higher, even more efficacious levels of attainment. But first, a necessary pause for some deeper definitions of how and why "Convertibles" are issued by companies in the first place, and how they develop their "heads I win, tails I don't lose" characteristics which are at the very heart of every Convertible strategy.

WHY Do Almost All Convertibles Hold Up Better Than Their Common Stocks In A Falling Market?

We have demonstrated that at Conversion Parity, the *maximum* decline that can be suffered by a Convertible when its common stock falls, is the exact percentage drop in the common, and no more, but that there is no *necessity* for the Convertible to suffer that same percentage drop. Indeed, it is a demonstrable fact that very few Convertibles decline to the maximum extent, or to Conversion Parity, when their respective common stocks suffer a serious decline, fully establishing the fact that well-situated Convertibles protect capital in down markets better than their respective common stocks—very often *far* better.

To understand one of the major reasons why a well-situated Convertible will fall more slowly than its common stock, we must first understand that a Convertible Bond or a Convertible Preferred Stock is "senior" to the common stock in any company's capitalization.

If you own shares of common stock, you are, to the extent of your ownership, a direct proprieter of the company —you *own* the company. As such, if the company fares well, building earnings, reinvesting earnings in new plant and equipment, developing new products, adding to working capital, the value of the company rises, and so, typically, does the market value of your common shares which represent the ownership of that increased value.

As an owner of the company, you are entitled to share with all other common stockholders any dividends that are declared by corporate management on the common stock, dividend payout normally rising with earnings, but also capable of being reduced or eliminated when earnings fall, or when the company has large cash needs in excess of its cash flow.

How Corporations Raise Money

At times, a company is expanding so fast that the money flowing in from earnings after taxes isn't enough to finance inventory, or necessary new plant and equipment, or other corporate needs. Or earnings may be lagging and normal corporate needs are in excess of available funds. Under such circumstances, a company may seek to raise the needed funds in four major ways, and we illustrate each below.

1. Sell more common stock. Example from Wall Street Journal, February 6, 1976.

Toledo Edison Will Offer Two Million Shares March 8

TOLEDO — Toledo Edison Co. said it plans to offer publicly two million common shares March 8. The stock has a current market value of nearly $50 million.

The offer, which the Ohio utility said it registered with the Securities and Exchange Commission, will be handled by underwriters headed by First Boston Corp. and Merrill Lynch, Pierce, Fenner & Smith Inc. Proceeds will be added to the concern's general funds and be used primarily to repay short-term notes issued for construction and to defray a part of the cost for such construction.

In September 1975, Toledo Edison raised $31.3 million when it sold 1.5 million common shares at $20.875 each. The utility had an average 9.7 million shares outstanding last year.

2. Borrow the money from a bank. Example from Wall Street Journal, January 29, 1976.

TransCanada Places $50 Million of Debt

By a WALL STREET JOURNAL Staff Reporter

TORONTO—TransCanada PipeLines Ltd. said it privately placed $50 million of five-year, 7¼% income debentures with its bankers.

A company official declined to identify the banks, but said they are Canadian chartered banks.

TransCanada said proceeds will be used to pay for its 1975 construction program and part of the 1976 program.

The company also reported its 1975 net income soared 45% to $66.3 million, or $1.65 a share, from the year-earlier $45.6 million, or $1.17 a share. Revenue jumped 62%, to $920.4 million from $567.9 million, Average common shares increased to 31.7 million from 28.7 million.

The natural gas pipeline concern's rate of return last year on its utility rate base rose to 9.8% from 8.6% in 1974. It was recently authorized by Canada's National Energy Board to earn a 10.2% return on its rate base.

3. Sell an issue of Bonds. Example from Wall Street Journal, February 6, 1976.

Texas Utilities Unit Planning to Auction $100 Million of Bonds

By a WALL STREET JOURNAL *Staff Reporter*

WASHINGTON—Texas Electric Service Co., one of three prime-rated electric utility borrowers, said it plans to auction $100 million of new 30-year first mortgage bonds.

The Fort Worth, Texas, concern will use proceeds to meet construction expenditures and for other corporate purposes. The proposed offer has been registered with the Securities and Exchange Commission. The sale is expected March 2.

In a previous debt offering last June, Texas Electric Service sold $50 million of new 30-year bonds with 8⅞% interest coupons.

Texas Electric Service and two other Texas Utilities Co. units are the few power concerns awarded the coveted triple-A bond rating by both Moody's and Standard & Poor's.

4. Sell an issue of Preferred Stock. Example from Wall Street Journal, January 29, 1976.

Kansas P&L Quickly Sells All 800,000 Preferred Shares

NEW YORK—Kansas Power & Light Co.'s 800,000 shares of new $2.33-dividend preferred stock sold out quickly at a price of $27.50 apiece, to return 8.44%, underwriters said.

Proceeds will be used to reduce short-term debt incurred in the utility's construction program.

Rated double-A by Moody's and single-A-plus by Standard & Poor's the shares were marketed through First Boston Corp., Dean Witter & Co. and associates.

The Corporate Bond

As noted, a new Bond issue states the amount of interest a buyer will receive per $100 face value held, and also states a maturity date when each $100 face value of Bond will be redeemed in cash by the company at its full face value.

The amount of the interest rate doesn't have anything to do with how much the company earns or does not earn, once a Bond is sold to investors. A company can triple its earnings in a year, and each $100 face value of Bond will still get only its stated interest, and no more. A company can also lose its earning power and go into deficit for a particular year, but no matter, the Bond holder must still get his stated interest in full, or there are provisions in the Bond "Indenture" (the contract between the company selling the Bonds, and the bondholders) which might turn the management of the company over to the bondholders, or which might allow them at least to elect a certain number of directors. Ultimately, if a company is unable to pay the interest on its Bonds, or redeem its Bonds at full face value on the stated maturity date, the company could be thrown into bankruptcy and its assets sold in order to satisfy the legally binding demands of the bondholders. And the bondholders would have to be paid off in full, principal and back interest due, before the common stockholders could get anything at all from this liquidation.

It is obvious from the above that a bondholder is *not* an owner of the company, as is a common stockholder. He is a *creditor* of the company, having, in effect, loaned it money, and expecting to receive his interest on that loan promptly and to be repaid in full at the stipulated time.

Corporate Preferred Stock

A preferred stock, typically, is next on the totem pole, just below the bondholder, but above the common stockholder, in ways we shall now describe. The preferred stock, just like the Bond, has a *stated rate of return,* which doesn't go up if company earnings improve, or go down if losses occur. The rate of return, in this case as a preferred dividend rather than interest paid on a bond, is *fixed.* So also, is the claim to assets of the company in the event the company goes into bankruptcy or liquidation. If preferred stock dividends are not paid, just as described with the Bond Indenture, there are typically provisions to protect the preferred stockholder as to the dividends due him and also the stipulated liquidating value of his preferred stock.

In the event the company goes into liquidation, the preferred stockholder must receive a stated amount (usually close to the selling price of the preferred stock when it was initially sold to investors) *before* the common stockholders can get anything. The holder of a preferred stock is a stockholder of the company and not a creditor, but since his dividend return is fixed, he does not share in any expanding prosperity for the company, other than to make more secure the regular payment of his stated dividend, and to make more remote any possibility that the company might get into financial difficulty.

"Straight" (that is, *non*convertible) corporate bonds and corporate preferred stocks can both be considered to be senior, fixed income securities, with their purchasers interested solely in their *return* on their investment in the form of interest or dividends, and the *safety* of their invested funds.

88

Price Fluctuations Of Senior Securities Compared With Price Fluctuations of Common Stocks

If the market price of a common stock fluctuates in accordance with the fortunes of the company and/or the general stock market, while the market price of a senior security fluctuates in accordance with the safety of yield and principal, then we would expect the market action of a senior security to be much more narrow and restricted than that of a common stock—and so it is. One other factor now enters, however, which imparts somewhat more movement to the senior security, and that is *the general level of interest rates.*

The interest rate is the "price" of money, and the varying fluctuations in the supply of, and the demand for, money, causes a rise and fall in that price, just as it would for any commodity, and the rise and fall is expressed in the entire range of *interest rates.* The latter part of 1974 saw, for example, very "tight" money, with the prime rate reaching over the 10% mark, and all interest rates climbing as a result, all along the line. One year later, in early-1976, money was much "easier" and the prime rate was down below 7% along, once again, with the entire range of interest rates moving down to lower levels.

The normal fluctuation which this engenders in the market price of senior securities, bonds and preferred stocks (and in this section we are talking about "straight" or nonconvertible, senior securities) occurs in the following manner. Let us say that we own a well-rated 7% corporate bond, selling in the marketplace in late-1974 at 70 to yield 10%. The relatively high yield (compared to recent years) was resulting from the competition of other existing, and newly-issued, senior securities, which had to provide yields of 9.5%, 10% and even higher, depending upon rating. (The greater the financial strength of the company, the better its rating and, therefore, the lower the interest rate at which it could normally sell new bonds or preferred stock to investors.)

This forced the market prices of all senior securities to come into line. In early-1976, however, interest rates were down all along the line because of changes in the supply/demand picture for money, and yields of about 8½% for long-term corporate senior securities were prevalent. Our 7% bond, which had been selling for 70 in late-1974 to yield *10%*, would now probably move up in price to almost 82 to yield about 8½%.

Some Common Stock, Bond, And Preferred Stock Price Ranges

The more restricted price movement for senior securities which results from what we have just described can be quickly appreciated by a sampling of price ranges during 1975 for the common stock and senior securities (Bonds or Preferred Stock) of the same company.

Thus, Atlanta Gas, a utility company, saw its common stock with a range of .... 14½ high—9½ low

This was a range of .... 52 %

Atlanta Gas "straight" (nonconvertible) bonds, the 8⅛s of 1998, in the same 1975 period, had a range of .... 87½ high—78¾ low

This was a range of .... 11 %

* * * * * *

General Electric, the "blue chip" giant, saw its
common stock with a 1975 range of . . . .
52⅞ high—32⅜ low
This was a range of . . . . 63 %
General Electric "straight" bonds, the 5.30s of
1992, in the same 1975 period, had a range of . . . .
78½ high—71½ low
This was a range of . . . . 10 %
* * * * * *

Mobil Oil, a large integrated oil company, saw
its common stock with a 1975 range of . . . .
48⅞ high—34⅛ low
This was a range of . . . . 43 %
Mobil Oil "straight" bonds, the 7⅜s of 2001, in
the same 1975 period, had a range of . . . .
93 high—81 low
This was a range of . . . . 15 %
* * * * * *

Northwest Industries, a conglomerate, saw its
common stock with a 1975 range of . . . .
35½ high—18⅞ low
This was a range of . . . . 88 %
Northwest Industries "straight" bonds, the 7½
of 1994, in the same 1975 period, had a range of . .
80½ high—68 low
This was a range of . . . . 18 %

91

We chose examples ranging from a conservative utility—Atlanta Gas—to a risk-taking conglomerate—Northwest Industries—and while there *was* greater fluctuation in the "straight" bonds of Northwest Industries as against that of Atlanta Gas, the fluctuations of the four Bond examples were all within a range of 11% to 18%, while the *common stock price ranges* of all four examples were in the 40% to 80% price ranges.

Thus we see clearly common stock, representing ownership of a company with all its attendant risks and rewards, with a very wide band of market fluctuation, while "straight" bonds, representing creditors of the company, with safety of interest and principal and the general level of interest rates the major factors, producing a much more restricted level of market fluctuation.

Several examples of preferred stock illustrate about the same level of comparative fluctuations compared with their respective common stocks, with a bit more range for the preferred stocks because of their relatively lower position on the totem pole compared with Bonds.

Thus, Crown Zellerbach, paper and lumber giant, saw its common stock with a 1975 range of ......
40⅝ high—24⅛ low
This was a range of .... 68 %
Crown Zellerbach $4.20 Preferred Stock, in the same 1975 period, had a range of 60 high—50 low
This was a range of .... 20 %

* * * * * *

Koppers Co., active in forest products, chemicals and road building, saw its common stock with a 1975 range of .... 37⅝ high—18¼ low

               This was a range of ... 106 %

Koppers Co. 4% Preferred Stock, in the same 1975 period, had a range of .... 54 high—42½ low

               This was a range of .... 27 %

* * * * * *

General Motors saw its common stock with a 1975 range of .... 59⅛ high—31¼ low

               This was a range of .... 89 %

General Motors $5 Preferred Stock, in the same 1975 period, had a range of .... 59 high—68¾ low

               This was a range of .... 16 %

Deere's $100 Million Of Convertible Debt Is Sold Out Quickly

By a WALL STREET JOURNAL Staff Reporter

NEW YORK—Despite the stiff terms, investors snapped up Deere & Co.'s $100 million of new 25-year convertible debentures priced at 100 with 5½% interest coupons.

That 5½% annual return is at least three percentage points less than the going rate on comparable nonconvertible bonds, dealers said. In addition, the equivalent price of Deere common stock obtained through conversion of the debentures is a sharp 16.18% premium above the current market value, they added.

Nevertheless, the single-A-rated debentures sold out quickly, primarily to institutional buyers. "There has been a prolonged scarcity of new convertible issues, particularly from such well-known and respected companies as Deere," one market specialist commented.

The debentures are convertible at the rate of one share for every $65.50 of debentures; yesterday, the common closed at $55.875 in New York Stock Exchange trading. Roughly 1.5 million new shares would be required to cover full conversion of the $100 million issue. Recently, about 30 million were outstanding.

At least 74% of the debentures are to be retired before final maturity in 2001 through a sinking fund, which begins operating in 1968.

Deere, a Moline, Ill., maker of farm and other equipment, will use the proceeds to reduce bank debt and for other purposes. Its sale was handled by Merrill Lynch, Pierce, Fenner & Smith Inc. and associates.

* * *

94

Now—The CONVERTIBLE Senior Security

That one news item tells us quite a bit about Convertibles! Thus:

"Despite the stiff terms, investors snapped up Deere & Co.'s $100 million of new 25-year convertible debentures priced at 100 with 5½% interest coupons.

"That 5½% annual return is at least three percentage points less than the going rate on corporate nonconvertible bonds, dealers said . . ."

Note that on a $100 million bond issue, a corporation finding it possible to market their bonds at a 5½% interest rate by adding a convertible feature, rather than 8½% if sold as a nonconvertible bond issue, saves the company 3% on $100,000,000 annually, or *$3 million each year.*

We have an important reason here why companies issue Convertibles in the first place, and added to this is the fact that at various times the sale of "straight" (nonconvertible) bonds becomes difficult for any company, making a convertible senior security issue—a Convertible Bond or a Convertible Preferred Stock—the issue of choice in raising new corporate funds.

Again quoting from the news item:

"In addition, the equivalent price of Deere common stock obtained through conversion of the debentures is a sharp 16.18% premium above the current market value," they added.

This figure is arrived at by further noting that "The debentures are convertible at the rate of one share for every $65.50 of debentures; yesterday, the common closed at $55.875 in New York Stock Exchange trading . . ."

Since each $65.50 of debenture can be converted into 1

common share when we divide $65.50 into $100.00 (coming to 1.526 shares) we arrive at the conversion rate *per $100 face value* of debenture bond, a much more meaningful conversion figure since bonds *trade* in $100 face value denominations on the Exchange and over-the-counter.

With the common stock selling at 55⅞, the Conversion Value of the new Convertible Bond, the Deere & Co. 5½s of 2001, is 55.875 x 1.526 or 85.26. The new Convertible Bond selling at *100* initially, to get the *premium over Conversion Value,* we divide the price of the Bond (100) by the Conversion Value (85.26) and we come up with the premium of 17.28%. The 16.18% premium noted in the Wall Street Journal article reflected a somewhat lower price for the Convertible Bond at that particular point, somewhere around the 99¼ level.

Thus, the issuance of new Convertibles, and we proceed immediately to highlight the fact that the market fluctuation of the new Deere & Co. Convertible 5½s of 2001 would be *much* different than if the issue had *not* been convertible, and had been sold to yield 8½% as noted.

The UPside

If Deere & Co. common stock, after sale of the issue, moved up 20 points from 55⅞ to 75⅞, a nonconvertible issue (issued at a yield of about 8½%) would have remained somewhere near the 100 mark, fluctuating to a minor degree for reasons previously noted.

The *convertible* issue would, of necessity, respond to a move by Deere common to 75⅞ by selling at *a minimum* of 115¾, for its straight Conversion Value at that price would be 75.875 x 1.526 which equals 115.78.

The DOWNside

Suppose now a severe general market slide ensued and Deere common dropped 20 points from 55⅞ to *35⅞*.

The nonconvertible issue would still show only moderate change responding almost solely to changes in the general level of interest rates. What would be the effect on the *Convertible* issue?

Let us first calculate the straight Conversion Value with Deere common at 35⅞. That Conversion Value would be 35.875 x 1.526, or 54.74. Would the Deere & Co. Convertible 5½s of 2001 *sell* at that straight Conversion Value of 54¾? Hardly, for at 54¾ the Bond would yield 10.04%, and *the status of the 5½s of 2001 a a senior security of Deere & Co. would now come into play,* the Bond having a prior claim to its interest payments before the common stock could get any dividends, and having the right to be paid off at full face value in the event of the company's dissolution before the common stock could get one cent.

At the upside level of 75⅞ for Deere common, the 5½s of 2001 had left its status as a senior security behind, and was responding solely to its conversion feature, for at 115¾ (that was its *minimum* price, it probably would have sold somewhat higher, at a premium) it was yielding only 4.75%, and its senior security status gave it little protection at such a level when nonconvertible issues were yielding 8½%.

At *35⅞* for Deere common, the 5½s of 2001 could not respond solely to its conversion feature because this would have meant a price of 54¾ and a yield of 10.4%, and its senior security status would have moved in to keep the Convertible at a considerably higher level than its straight

Conversion Value.

How much higher the Convertible issue would have sold would have typically depended on *two* factors. The first factor would be its normal investment value as a straight (nonconvertible) bond, typically allowing the bond to sell at least at a price where it would be yielding about 8½%, if that is what straight bonds of that quality were yielding at the time. This would enable the Convertible issue, in this instance, to stop its decline at least at 64¾, where it was yielding 8½%.

But the second factor would also operate strongly, and this factor would be embodied in the Bond's long-term conversion privilege, the ability to convert each $100 face value of Bond into 1.526 shares of Deere & Co. common stock until the year *2001!*

Many analysts of Convertibles insist upon tagging a Convertible with an "Investment Value" figure, which is the price at which the Bond would sell on yield alone, as if it were a nonconvertible issue. But the conversion right never ceases to operate, almost never ceases to have *some* market value built into the price of the Convertible.

Thus, it is a much more useful approach, in this writer's view, to carefully examine the prior behavior of an existing Convertible during periods of market reaction when its common stock sold to lower levels. Usually, it is possible to average out the premium over Conversion Value at which such Convertibles sold during a number of prior periods of lower levels for its common stock, and to arrive at a figure which this writer calls the "Estimated Support Level." We have already, in a previous chapter, made reference to this figure as a part of the statistical tables of the R.H.M. Convertible Survey.

This "ESL" figure takes into account the previous areas of support during declining markets and the current and anticipated interest rate level, which affects the "nonconvertible" senior security aspect. The significance of the "Estimated Support Level" figure is that it gives you some measure of the degree of downside risk in purchasing a specific Convertible. Thus, if a Convertible is selling at 82 and the Estimated Support Level is 74, we know that we are dealing with an approximate 10% risk factor in making a purchase.

If the same Convertible, on the other hand, is selling at *110,* having been drawn up to this higher level on Conversion Value as the common stock moved ahead, we know that the Estimated Support Level is still about 74 and the risk factor is now about 33%.

To summarize, finally, why well-situated Convertibles hold up better than their common stocks in a falling market, very often *far* better, we find the reasons in the twin facts that the value of the Convertible as a "straight" (nonconvertible) senior security comes into play as the decline proceeds, *plus* the value of the long-term conversion privilege into the common stock. Add these two factors together and you have a very solid "floor" under a Convertible in a falling market, which fact was demonstrated at length in preceding pages in a most specific manner.

"Called" Convertibles

In pursuit of their own needs, companies that issue Convertible Bonds and Convertible Preferred Stocks give themselves the option of "Calling" the issues for repayment. Typically, such "Call" provisions are a few points above par, or the price at issuance, and are utilized by a company when they wish to, in most cases, force conversion into common stock. The "force" arises when a Convertible is selling, say, at 180, forced up to that level by a rising common stock, and the entire issue of this Convertible is "Called" at, say, 104. No investor is going to turn his Convertible into the company for $104 when it is worth $180 in terms of the market value of the common stock for which it can be exchanged. So the investor either sells his Convertible in the open market, or actually converts it into common stock.

When a Convertible is selling far above the "Call" price, it is usually the task of the "arbitrageur" to convert into common stock. Bids for the Convertible are set fractionally under the actual market value of the Bond or Preferred Stock, and the seller is happy to allow the arbitrageur a small profit to avoid the bother of actually "converting." The arbitrageur buys the Convertible and simultaneously sells common stock short, later converting into common stock to make delivery. He is usually happy to take ½-point or thereabouts to perform this service.

The only time a Convertible "Call" becomes a problem is when a company chooses to undertake this when the Convertible is still close enough to par to be selling a a premium. Thus, a Convertible may be selling at, say, 124, when its actual Conversion Value is 118, and as soon as the "Call" is announced, the premium disappears so that the Convertible drops to straight Conversion Value at 118, for a loss of six points.

We do not view this as a large problem at all, since the great majority of "Calls" come when the Convertible is far above par and selling at 0 premium anyway. And an additional safeguard is always to diversify holdings as widely as possible, so that such individual circumstances are not significant. Such investment services as The R.H.M. Convertible Survey, and other financial and advisory services, report on "Calls" as soon as they are announced, alerting holders to the necessity of either converting into common stock, or selling in the open market.

The publisher, R.H.M. Press, has agreed to make available to the reader, at no extra charge, a Special Supplement, giving the author's current and completely updated analysis and statistical presentation of the entire list of currently outstanding Convertible Bonds and Convertible Preferred Stocks, including a statistical presentation of Euro-Convertible Bonds and Convertibles with Call Option Hedge Potential, in accordance with the description of these areas of "Opportunities In Convertibles" set forth in this book.

To receive this Special Supplement, important to following current opportunities, send your name and address—be sure to include zip—to:

R.H.M. Press   Dept. 85
840 Willis Avenue
Albertson, Long Island
New York 11507

There will be no charge for this Special Supplement.

Discount and Deep-Discount Convertibles

We have been writing up to this point of the many superior opportunities which develop with Convertibles selling at, or near, Conversion Parity, at 0 or near-0 premiums. Does this mean that Convertibles at 30%, 40%, 60%, even 100% premiums over Conversion Value are to be ignored? Not unless you want to pass up some handsome profits at minor risk!

When a Convertible breaks away from its common stock during a down market, refusing at a certain strategic point to fall as fast as its common stock, it will still continue to fall, though at a reduced percentage rate compared with the common stock. But the percentage rate of fall for the Convertible will continue to diminish until, at a certain point, it becomes virtually motionless.

It is the combined value of the now heightened yield (the lower the price of the Convertible Bond or Preferred, the higher the yield) plus the value of the long-term Call on the common stock, which finally brings the Convertible decline to a halt.

At such a point, some additional modest decline could certainly take place, particularly if, say, the entire bond market slips lower in response to firming interest rates. But in many cases the upside potential at such "bottoms" far exceeds whatever modest risks remain, and the Convertible can become an excellent haven for funds in a perhaps doubtful and worrisome market. In such cases one can be enjoying a high yield for sheltered funds with the potential for capital gain still quite alive if fears go unrealized and, instead, a market *rally* takes place.

As an example of this one can look at the R.H.M. Convertible Survey issue dated 12-26-75 and find Budd Co. 5⅞s of 1994 selling at 58 with the common at 9⅜. Each $100 face value of Bond is convertible into 4.545 shares of Budd common, making the Conversion Value 9.375 x 4.545 or 42.6. We divide the Convertible price (58) by the Conversion Value (42.6) and arrive at the premium over Conversion Value, which is a substantial 36%.

Why ignore such an opportunity? At 58, the 5⅞s of 1994 are yielding 10.1%, and upon any recovery in the stock the Convertible Bond would certainly show *some* appreciation.

Good yield, a large measure of downside safety, and potential for later capital appreciation are the hallmarks of a well-situated "Discount Convertible," the term "Discount" referring to its distance from par (100 for a Bond), and its distance also from Conversion Value.

As January 1976 came into view, there was *not* the decline so many expected in December 1975 but, rather, a vigorous rise. Budd Co. common rose sharply from 9⅜ to a February 1976 high of 16⅛. At 16⅛, Conversion Value of the 5⅞s of 1994 was now 16.125 x 4.545 or 73.28. The Convertible Bond still retaining some premium at this high, actually sold at 80.

Not only had the Budd Co. Convertible Bond provided a 10.1% yield in December 1975, and acted as a good haven for funds while the market gave more evidence as to its near-term direction, but in moving from 58 to 80, the Budd Co. Convertible Bond produced a very welcome 38% profit in just two months!

"Deeper" Discount Convertibles

We go back another year to another point of pessimism and fear—December 1974, at what proved to be the bottom of the 1973-1974 market collapse. Here, from the R.H.M. Convertible Survey issue of 12-27-74 we find Tyler Corp. 5s of 1993 selling at 62⅝, with the common stock at 13½. The Conversion Rate was 2.740 so the Conversion Value was 13.5 x 2.740, or only 37.0. The Convertible Bond was selling at a 69% premium over Conversion Value.

Yielding 8.0% and promising excellent downside protection at this level, the Convertible also rewarded its buyers, in the 1975 recovery of its common stock, by moving up to 106, an advance of 69%.

Yes, the percentage profit would have been greater in December 1974 if you would have purchased Tyler Corp. *common* instead of the Convertible Bond. But the safety factor was *much* higher for the Convertible Bond in December 1974, and who could have guaranteed that Tyler Corp. common was not going to suffer a further serious decline? Again, the virtues of the "Discount Convertible."

A STILL Deeper Discount Convertible

To demonstrate that even a 100% premium over Conversion Value should not dissuade us from examining the possibilities of a profit opportunity, consider the case, from the same issue of the R.H.M. Convertible Survey, 12-27-74, of Allen Group 11½ of 1994. Each $100 face value of Bond was Convertible into 7.143 shares of common. With the common at a lowly $4, Conversion Value was 4.0 x 7.143 or 28.6, but the Convertible Bond was selling far above that Conversion Value, at 64½, which represented a premium over Conversion Value of *126%*.

If one's eye slid over to the Bond Yield column in the statistical section, one could quickly find cause to take a closer look at this situation, for at 64½ for the Bond, an 11½% interest rate worked out to a yield of *17.8%*.

A look at the Balance Sheet would reveal a sufficiently sound situation (Walter B. Kissinger, president of Allen Group, is a competent industrialist, and brother of famed Henry Kissinger) so the 17.8% yield was not a prelude to bankruptcy and was actually a quite safe return, in this writer's opinion.

Came improving business for Allen Group as the Citizens Band radios caught fire in the country (the company is an important producer of antennas for these radios) and the common shot up, taking the Convertible Bond with it to a high of 126.

17.8% yield and a 95% profit. Deep discount Convertibles evidently merit an investor's close attention at *any* stage of the market cycle, but particularly when doubts and fears are widespread. At such time, moving into the deep discount Convertibles of soundly financed companies can prove rewarding in the direction of high yields, downside safety and potential capital appreciation, along the lines just described.

The Convertible Hedge

The basic logic of the Convertible, which gives it all of its attraction, is grounded in the concept we have demonstrated in many previous pages that while, at Conversion Parity, a Convertible *must* go up at least as much as its common stock in equal dollar amounts, should the common stock turn to the downside instead of moving up, the Convertible *cannot* suffer a greater loss than the common stock, dollar-for-dollar invested, does not have to suffer *as* great a loss, and, indeed, typically holds up better than the common stock, often far better.

This being so, and it is so without question, many promising profit possibilities open up for the informed investor, grouped under the general heading of the "Convertible Hedge." Once again this writer draws upon some decades of experience with the comings and goings of such Hedge positions to state that the vast majority of investors, and much of the professional brokerage fraternity as well, pay little or no attention to such Hedge positions. We state frankly that we are amazed at such indifference and do not have the answer after all these years as to why it is so. But this "indifference" means that those investors who *do* pay attention to the profit potential of the Convertible Hedge in all its varieties of possibilities can be much more greatly rewarded than if there were general awareness. For then the potential would narrow through competition, even though with so many hundreds of Convertibles actively trading, ample opportunities would still be present. The fact is, however, that attention paid to the Convertible

Hedge is sufficiently small so that opportunities are plentiful and rewarding, as we shall soon see.

We Start With A Hypothetical Example

Let us assume a simple Conversion Rate by which each $100 face value of XYZ 6% Convertible Bond is convertible into 2 shares of XYZ common, and that the XYZ Convertible Bond is selling at 100, and XYZ common is selling at 50, direct Conversion Parity. The Convertible Bond must keep at least exact pace with the common stock on the upside, but recent market history had demonstrated that when XYZ common fell to 25 in a declining market, the XYZ Convertible Bond had not declined to its straight Conversion Value of 50, at which price it would have been yielding 12%, but had held up at 75 where it yielded 8%.

A previous common—Convertible price relationship at a low need not necessarily be repeated during a subsequent market decline, but this happens often enough, and closely enough so that we may assume this for purposes of the explanation of the Convertible Hedge which we shall now describe.

Giving a quick definition, a Convertible Hedge involves being "Long" the Convertible and "Short" the common stock, in varying proportions to seek different objectives.

Short-Selling

We are all familiar with what it means to take a "Long" position in a security. We purchase the security at one market level, hoping and expecting that the security will advance in price so that when we sell it, we will have a profit. Thus, you buy 100 shares of XYZ common at 25 and, hopefully, sell it at 50.

In "Short-Selling" you do exactly the opposite, and let us use the same prices. We *first* sell 100 shares of XYZ common "short" at 50, and then later buy it back at 25 to complete the transaction, earning a handsome profit by this downside movement in the common stock. When we "sold" the common stock originally, we *did not own it*. We hoped and expected that it would go down in price, whereupon we would buy it at the lower price to nail down our profit.

Upon selling "short," our broker would have borrowed a certificate for 100 shares of XYZ common from another broker to make delivery to the buyer. When you completed the transaction by buying the stock at the happily lower level, he used that purchased stock to return to the firm he had borrowed it from, leaving everything quite even, but you with a good profit! Many investors regard "short-selling" as mysterious and even, peculiarly enough, reprehensible. This very probably is why so little attention is paid to the Convertible Hedge, which necessarily includes short-selling, but let this writer assure the reader that the securities industry has facilitated short-selling throughout its career as a necessary ingredient in creating adequate markets for buyers and sellers, that there is nothing mysterious about it, and certainly nothing reprehensible in any manner! On to our first example of a Convertible Hedge.

The Half-Hedge

Each $100 face value of the XYZ 6% Convertible Bond is convertible into 2 shares of XYZ common stock, so that $1,000 face value of Bond is convertible into 20 shares, and $10,000 face value of Bond is convertible into 200 shares of XYZ common.

In *any* Convertible *Half*-Hedge, you buy X amount of the Convertible and sell Short ½ the amount of common stock for which the Convertible can be exchanged. If we, then, went "Long" $10,000 face amount of XYZ Convertible Bond, and that amount of Bond was convertible into *200* shares of common stock, we would sell short *100* shares of XYZ common. Using the market prices of 100 for the Bond and 50 for the common, exact Conversion Parity, we would have the following Hedge position:

Long $10,000 face amount of XYZ
Convertible Bond at 100;   cost........$10,000

Short 100 shares XYZ common
at 50;   cost........   0

The reason for stating the "cost" of the short-sale as 0 is one of the large attractions of the Convertible Hedge, stemming from a Federal Reserve Board margin requirement ruling which states that on a short-sale of a common stock, when there are securities in the same account *convertible* within 90 days into the securities sold short, without restriction other than the payment of money, then no margin need be put up to carry the short position in the common. This means you need not put up any margin at all to carry the short position in the common stock when you are simultaneously holding a Convertible security which can be exchanged for at least that amount of stock. The great importance of this will shine through after we consider the various results which can eventuate with our Half-Hedge position as given above.

The UPside

XYZ common doubles in the market from 50 to 100. The 100 shares of common stock which had enjoyed a market value of $5,000 at 50 now have a market value of $10,000. If you were "long" the common, you would be counting up a $5,000 profit, but remember that *you had sold the stock short,* so you have a $5,000 *loss* rather than a profit.

But the Convertible Bond is ready to gallop to the rescue. At 100 for the common stock, the Convertible Bond, each $100 face value convertible into 2 shares of common stock, must have a market value of 100 x 2, or *$200.* The original $10,000 face value of Bond had a market value of $10,000 with the Bond at 100, and with the Bond now at *200,* the market value is *$20,000* for a profit of $10,000.

A loss of $5,000 on the short-sale of the common stock;

A profit of $10,000 on the purchase of the Convertible Bond;

You have a net profit on this Hedge position of *$5,000.*

It only takes a moment to realize that at *any* upside point for the common stock, your profit on the Long position in the Convertible Bond will necessarily and always be at least twice the loss on the Short position in the common stock. In effect, the Half-Hedge taken at Conversion Parity gives you a 50% net Long position on the upside, at *any* upside point for the common stock.

The DOWNside

XYZ common does not double in price from 50 to 100, but *falls* in price from 50 to 25.

The 100 shares of common stock which had
been sold short at 50 now have a profit of 25
points on 100 shares, or a profit of $2,500

The Convertible Bond, in line with the assumptions made
at the beginning of this description of the Convertible Half-
Hedge, has not dropped all the way to its straight Conversion Value, from 100 to 50, but has held up at 75. At 75,
there is a 25-point loss on $10,000 face value of Bond, or
a loss of $2,500.

The gain on the short-sale of the common cancels out
the loss on the Long position in the Convertible Bond, and
we have avoided any net loss at all on the downside.

"Heads I Win—Tails I Don't Lose"

The statement in the above heading is completely accu-
rate in the context of what we have just described. A Half-
Hedge position had to produce a profit if XYZ common
went *up,* but produced no loss if XYZ common went *down.*
"Heads I win" (the stock moves up), "Tails I don't lose"
(the stock moves down).

Now let us go back to the importance we ascribed to not
having to put up any cash to carry the short position in the
common when we simultaneously held the Convertible.
Looking at the Long position in the Convertible Bond, and
recognizing the low-risk nature of this Hedge position, we
would want to leverage the potential by using as much borrowed funds as possible. Therefore, since current margin
regulations, as we write, permit the use of 50% margin in
carrying Bonds, we put up only $5,000 in cash to carry the
$10,000 in XYZ Convertible Bonds, and nothing at all to
carry the short position in the common, so that our total

Cash outlay for this position is $5,000.

If our expectation that XYZ common would go *up* proved correct and the common stock went from 50 to 100, the $5,000 net profit we described above would have developed on only a *$5,000 cash investment,* or a 100% return on invested capital. If the result shown took, say, six months, this would be an annualized return of 200%—all on a modest risk, close-to-0 risk, transaction.

The Full-Hedge

Where the Half-Hedge is aimed at upside profits (on the downside you only want to minimize loss as close to 0 as possible) the *Full*-Hedge is aimed at *down*side profits. The fascinating thing about the Full-Hedge, taken at Conversion Parity, is that it *is* totally, absolutely riskless, and with much more profit potential than is realized even by the too few professionals and general investors somewhat familiar with the mechanics of the Full-Hedge. Almost everywhere we have found an insufficient appreciation of what the Full-Hedge can accomplish and, of course, among the great bulk of average investors, there is that total lack of awareness which applies to the entire Convertibles field.

The Full-Hedge itself involves no complications whatever. Instead of selling short *one-half* the amount of common stock for which your Convertible Long position can be exchanged, you sell short the *full amount* of the common stock.

Put in terms of our hypothetical example of XYZ Corp., where $10,000 face amount of XYZ 6% Convertible Bond is convertible into 200 shares of XYZ common, you sell short, not 100 shares of common, as in the Half-Hedge, but *200* shares of XYZ common.

Again using the market prices of 100 for the Bond and 50 for the common, the Full-Hedge taken at exact Conversion Parity, we would have the following Hedge position:

Long $10,000 face amount of XYZ 6%
Convertible Bond at 100;   cost........$10,000
Short 200 shares XYZ common
at 50;   cost........   0

The UPside

XYZ common doubles in the market from 50 to 100. On the short-sale of 200 shares of common at 50, you now have a 50-point loss on 200 shares, or a loss of $10,000

But at 100 for the common, the Convertible Bond must sell at 2 x 100, or 200, and the $10,000 face amount of Bond is now worth $20,000, or a gain of $10,000

Gain has cancelled loss, and it is obvious that for *any* upside move in the common, gain in the Convertible Bond would *always* cancel out the loss on the short-sale of the common, for at any point on the upside the Convertible Bond could always be converted into the 200 shares of common stock to make delivery, at 0 net loss.

A Full-Hedge taken at Conversion Parity is, by definition, completely riskless on the upside, resulting in no gain, and no loss.

The DOWNside

Here, now, is where the Full-Hedge begins to shine. The

113

first thing to realize is that *at worst,* no net loss at all is possible. This "worst" would be the Convertible Bond declining at exactly the rate of the common stock, declining to straight Conversion Parity at the lower levels. If this took place, we could have the following situation:

XYZ common does not double in price from 50 to 100, but *falls* in price from 50 to 25.

The 200 shares of common stock which had
been sold short at 50 now have a profit of 25
points on 200 shares, or a profit of . . . . $ 5,000

If the Convertible Bond now dropped to its
straight Conversion Value of 25 x 2, or 50, the
$10,000 face amount of Convertible Bond would
now be worth only $5,000, a loss of . . . . $ 5,000

Since a Convertible cannot sell *below* its straight Conversion Value, this $5,000 loss on the Convertible would be the *maximum* that could be suffered, and if the maximum did eventuate, gain would always cancel loss.

But the entire logic of the well-situated Convertible is that it does *not* decline at the same rate as the common stock, as we have demonstrated repeatedly in previous pages. And, to the extent that a Convertible declines more slowly than the common on the downside, *the Full-Hedge produces a profit.*

To get some idea of what that profit might be, let us take again the assumption that if XYZ common dropped from 50 to 25, the XYZ 6% Convertible Bond would not fall from 100 to its straight Conversion Value of 50, but would actually hold at 75. The comparative gain and loss would then work out as follows:

XYZ Common has dropped from 50 to 25.
The 200 shares of XYZ common which had been
sold short at 50 now show a profit of 25 points
on 200 shares, or a gain of . . . . $ 5,000

XYZ 6% Convertible Bonds have dropped at
the same time from 100 to 75, so there is a 25-
point drop on $10,000 face value of Bonds,
or a loss of . . . . $ 2,500

Our net gain of $2,500 on this transaction has been
earned on a total investment of $10,000 for the Long posi-
tion in the Bonds with nothing at all needed to carry the
short position. Again, because of the totally riskless nature
of the position, we utilize the full 50% margin, so actual
cash outlay is $5,000.

A profit of $2,500 on a $5,000 investment is 50% and
again, if the transaction took six months to come to a conclusion, this would represent an annualized profit of 100%.

From "XYZ Corp." To The
Real World of Convertibles

The Half-Hedge

From the figures above we have seen that at Conversion
Parity and utilizing a *Half-Hedge* where one buys X amount
of the Convertible and sells short ½ x the number of
shares of common for which the Convertible can be exchanged upon conversion, we enjoy, in effect, a 50% net
long position on the upside. This can work out to a large
percentage profit indeed when we get a significant upside
move in the common stock, and when we utilize the full
50% margin to carry the Convertible because of the

lowered-risk quality of the position. On the downside, if the common stock falls twice as fast as the Convertible on a percentage basis, we have seen that the loss in the Convertible will be offset completely by the gain on the short-sale of the common stock.

In moving over to "the real world of Convertibles" instead of our examples of "XYZ Corp." we do not have a distant move to make; we need only go back a few pages to our chapter on "The MOST Important Contribution of the Convertible." Toward the end of that chapter we gave a few examples of Convertibles selling close to Conversion Parity which, quite typically, *had* to rise as much, or almost as much, as their common stocks on any upside move in the common, but which promised to hold up better than their common stocks on any downside moves because of the combination of their investment value as senior securities *plus* their long-term conversion privileges.

We then went directly to the reality of the 1973 sinking spell in the stock market, which thereafter went on to the 1974 disaster, and gave the actual results of the percentage decline in each Convertible as measured against the actual percentage decline in their respective common stocks from November 1972, close to the highs, to the August 1973 bottom, the first step in the 1973-1974 market debacle.

In the case of Belden Corp., the common stock dropped 25.5% while the Belden Convertible Bond, the 8's of 1990, dropped only 11.1% in exactly the same November 1972-August 1973 period. The common stock had dropped 2.29 times faster than the Convertible.

With the example of Jostens Inc., the common stock dropped 45.5% and the Convertible Bond 21.3%. The common stock had dropped 2.13 times faster than the Convertible.

With the example of Kirsch Company, the common stock dropped 55.1% and the Convertible Bond 26.0%. The common stock had dropped 2.12 times faster than the Convertible.

With the example of Wayne Mfg., the common stock dropped 32% and the Convertible Bond 14%. The common stock had dropped 2.28 times faster than the Convertible.

Finally, in the example we gave for a Convertible Preferred Stock, with Occidental Petroleum, the common stock dropped 31.4% while the Convertible Preferred Stock dropped 12.9%. The common stock had dropped 2.43 times faster than the Convertible.

The Example Of Belden Corp. 8's Of 1990

It will be useful to run through the actual "numbers" involved in this specific "Half-Hedge" position for our first example of Belden 8's of 1990 to demonstrate arithmetically that when a common stock falls twice as fast as the Convertible on the downside, the profit on the short-sale of the common must at least balance out the loss on the Long position in the Convertible. Here is Belden Corp. common in November selling at 27½ with the Convertible Bond, the 8's of 1990, selling at 112½. A Half-Hedge involves being "Long" x amount of Convertible and "Short" x the amount of common stock the Convertible can receive upon conversion.

In this case, let us assume that we purchase (go "Long") $10,000 face amount of the Belden 8's of 1990. Since the Bond is selling at 112½, this is an outlay of *$11,250.*

In November 1972 each $100 face value of the Belden Corp. 8's of 1990 was convertible into exactly 4.0 shares of Belden common. Hence, $10,000 face amount of Bond was convertible into *400* shares of common stock.

Since this is a *Half*-Hedge, we sell short one-half that total, or 200 shares of Belden common at its then price of 27½. 200 shares at 27½ comes to *$5,500,* but we need put up no funds to carry this short position since we have previously referred to Federal Reserve Regulations which hold that on the short-sale of a security where there are securities in the same account convertible within 90 days into the securities sold short without restriction other than the payment of money (which certainly applies in every detail to a Convertible) *no* margin need be put up to carry the short position in the common.

118

Our total cash outlay up to this point, then, is the $11,250 to carry the Long position in $10,000 face amount of Belden 8's of 1990. (The use of margin here will come later.)

Comes August 1973 and we find Belden common down to *20¾*. The stock has fallen from 27½ to 20¾, down 6¾ points. On 200 shares, this is a profit of 200 x 6.75, or *$1,350*.

In exactly the same time period, November 1972 - August 1973, the Belden Convertible 8's of 1990 have fallen from 112½ to 100.0, down 12½ points. On $10,000 face amount of Bonds, this comes to a loss of *$1,250*.

The gain on the short sale of the common
has been ....$ 1,350

The loss on the "Long" position in the
Convertible Bond has been ....$ 1,250

It is not necessary to go through the other examples. *Wherever* the common stock has declined at least twice as fast as the Convertible on the downside, the Half-Hedge position of Long x amount of Convertible and Short ½ x the number of shares of common for which the Convertible can be exchanged upon conversion ensures that the loss in the Convertible position will be fully balanced out by the gain on the short-sale in the common.

Having demonstrated that the Convertible Half-Hedge is our insurance policy on the downside, let us remind readers that the purpose of the Half-Hedge position is to gain net profits on an *upside* move in the common.

Thus, assume that after November 1973, Belden Corp. common had not gone *down,* but had gone *up,* say from

119

27½ to 37½. At 37½ there would be a ten-point loss on the short-sale of 200 shares of common stock at 27½. Ten points on 200 shares is a loss of *$2,000*.

But at 37½ for Belden common, each $100 face amount of the Belden Convertible must be worth a minimum of 37.5 x 4, or 150. The Long position in $10,000 face amount of the Convertible Bond purchased for $11,250 is now worth $15,000 with the Bond at 150, for a gain of *$3,750*.

A gain of $3,750 and a loss of $2,000 and we come up with a net gain of *$1,750*.

Utilizing full 50% margin on the Convertible Long position, our actual cash outlay would have been half of $11,250, or $5,625, and the $1,750 profit would have been a 31% *gain* on only a moderate upside move in the common stock. If the move had taken, say, 6 months, the annualized return would be *62%*.

The Half-Hedge Convertible position had fully protected against downside loss but had permitted substantial upside gains. And if we went through each of the examples cited of the Convertibles of Jostens Inc., Kirsch Company, Wayne Mfg. and Occidental Petroleum, we would come to exactly the same conclusions because the Convertible "arithmetic" does not vary.

To tie up a few loose ends, we have omitted commissions throughout for the sake of clarity, but they would have only a slight effect on the outcome of any significant move in the common. Further, carrying the Long position in the Convertible at 50% margin would entail the usual margin interest charges. But in the case of Belden, for example, the Belden Corp. 8's of 1990 were yielding 7.1% at 112½, and with only 50% of the position subject to margin interest charges, which vary with the general interest level but are typically 6, 7 or 8%, the interest charges would be more than offset by the interest paid on the Bond during the holding period.

Further, in carrying a short position on the common stock, one is debited for any *dividends* paid on the common stock during the holding period of the short position, but the excess of the Convertible Bond interest over the margin interest offsets much of this in the case of Belden Corp., and in so many cases where the Convertible yield is far above the yield on the common, this factor becomes quite negligible.

The Convertible Half-Hedge, indeed, can be, in our opinion, *so* productive of substantial gains as described that none of the factors just discussed loom large in any sense. On the downside, in these positions, risk is much lower, or even down to the 0 level. On the upside, we have an actual 50% net Long position at any upside gain for the common stock when the position is taken at Conversion Parity. If a premium of 2% or 5% or 10% obtains for the Convertible upon the taking of a Half-Hedge position, this does no more than reduce the anticipated gain in a quite minor matter.

The Full-Hedge

Recalling that the Full-Hedge is aimed at profits with a *down*side movement of the common stock, and is achieved by selling short the *full* amount of common stock for which the Convertible can be exchanged, let us run through the same Convertible "arithmetic" which we used in describing the *Half*-Hedge with our first example, Belden Corp. 8s of 1990. Recall that in November 1972, Belden common was selling at 27½ with the Belden Convertible Bond selling at 112½. Each $100 face value of the Bond was convertible into 4 shares of common stock. With the common selling at 27½, the Conversion Value was 4 x 27.5 or 110. With the Bond selling at 112½, the premium over Conversion Value was negligible so, for all practical purposes, the Convertible Bond of Belden Corp. was selling at Conversion Parity.

Step No. 1: We buy $10,000 face amount of the Belden Corp. 8s of 1990 at 112½ for an outlay of $11,250

Step No. 2 (accomplished simultaneously): We sell short 400 shares of Belden Corp. common stock at 27½, for an outlay of 0

Remember that according to the Federal Reserve Board margin regulation previously referred to, when one is Long a Convertible security and one has sold short the corresponding common stock, one need not put up anything to carry the short position.

Remember also, that where our *Half*-Hedge position in Belden Corp. required us to sell short *one-half* the amount of common stock for which the Convertible could be exchanged, the *Full*-Hedge requires that we sell short the *full* amount of such common stock, in this case 400 shares of Belden common.

August 1973 rolls around with the drastic decline in the market—the initial blow on the downside—and we find Belden common down to 20¾ and the Convertible 8s of 1990 down to 100.

The common stock has fallen from 27½ to 20¾, down 24.5%.

The Convertible Bond has fallen from 112½ to 100, down 11.1%.

In dropping 6¾ points from 27½ to 20¾, the short-sale of 400 shares of Belden common has delivered a profit of 400 x 6.75 or $2,700

In dropping 12½ points from 112½ to 100, the Long position in $10,000 face amount of Belden 8s of 1990 has suffered a loss of 12½ points or $1,250

or a Gross Profit of $1,450

Since Hedge positions minimize risk, we utilize the full extent of margin applicable. In this case, since no margin at all has been put for the common stock short position (as was true also with the Half-Hedge position) we have only the $11,250 involved with the Convertible Bond to consider. Taking the full 50% margin, we need put up only $5,625 to carry our Full-Hedge as described.

A gross profit of $1,450 on a cash outlay of $5,625 comes to a profit of 25.77% in the 9 months the position was carried, or 34.36% on an annualized basis.

Since, taken at Conversion Parity, a Full-Hedge is *completely riskless,* an annualized return of 34% must be deemed a remarkable accomplishment. Yet, to their detriment, the Convertible Hedge, both Half-Hedge and Full-

Hedge, is almost completely ignored by the vast majority of investors.

A Full-Hedge In Occidental Petroleum
$3.60 Convertible Preferred

In our example of Belden 8s of 1990 there was only a 2.2% premium over Conversion Value, leading to our statement that the Convertible Bond, for all practical purposes, was selling at Conversion Parity. How is the Full-Hedge (or Half-Hedge, for that matter) affected by a higher premium over Conversion Value? This is an important question because if we are restricted only to 0 premiums, or close to 0 premiums, our possible horizons for establishing such positions are narrowed.

In actuality, we need have no such concern about shrinking horizons, for moderate premiums over Conversion Value in no way deter fruitful positions of every type in well-positioned Convertibles. To demonstrate this, let us look at the example previously outlined of the Occidental Petroleum $3.60 Convertible Preferred where an 11% premium over Conversion Value obtained.

In November 1972 Occidental Petroleum Common was selling at 13⅛ and the $3.60 Convertible Preferred Stock at 46½. Each share of the Preferred was convertible into 3.191 shares of common stock at any time. 13.125 x 3.191 equals 41.88, while the Convertible was selling at 46.50, so the premium over Conversion Value was 46.50 divided by 41.88 (Convertible Price divided by Conversion Value) to give us 11.10%.

Setting up a Full-Hedge position, we buy 100 shares of Occidental Petroleum $3.50 Convertible

Preferred at 46½ for an outlay of $4,650
We sell short the full amount of common stock
for which the 100 shares of Convertible Preferred
can be exchanged, or 320 shares at 13⅛ for
an outlay of   0
 In August 1973 we find Occidental Petroleum has
dropped from 13⅛ to 9, while the Occidental Petroleum
$3.60 Convertible Preferred has, in exactly the same period
of time, dropped from 46½ to 40½. The results are as
follow:
 In dropping 4⅛ points from 13⅛ to 9, the
short-sale of 320 shares of Occidental Petroleum
common has delivered a profit of 320 x 4.125 or . . $1,320
 In dropping 6 points from 46½ to 40½, the
Long position in 100 shares of Occidental
Petroleum $3.60 Convertible Preferred has
suffered a loss of 6 points or . . . . $ 600
       or a Gross Profit of . . . . $ 720
 Once again utilizing the full available margin, we have
put up only 50% of the $4,650 for the Convertible Pre-
ferred position, or $2,325.
 A gross profit of $720 on a cash outlay of $2,325 comes
to a profit of 30.96% in the 9 months the position was
carried, or 41.28% on an annualized basis.
 The 11% premium on the Convertible when the position
was established, not only did not prevent an appreciable
downside profit, but produced a larger profit than that enjoyed by the near-0 Convertible premium position in our
example of the Belden Convertible Bonds, because the Convertible Preferred of Occidental Petroleum held up better,
relative to the common stock, than the Belden Convertible.

Where the Belden Convertible would work more efficiently in a Full-Hedge because of its near-0 premium, would be in an *upside* move of the common stock. Here, at straight Conversion Parity, a Full-Hedge produces 0 loss on the upside, while an 11% premium over Conversion Value eventually works out to an 11% loss on the upside. We say, eventually, because premiums do not vanish immediately, but shrink only gradually as the upside direction persists. Thus, in the Full-Hedge position described above for Occidental Petroleum, *had* Occidental Petroleum common moved up instead of down, a minor loss would have begun to build up as the premium for the Convertible diminished.

The 11% net loss on an extensive upside move in the common stock would still mark this Full-Hedge as a "much more to gain than to lose" position—the downside profit potential being far larger than any possible upside loss— but if one did wish to eliminate loss entirely here, one could take a *90% Hedge* instead of a *100% Hedge* to compensate for that 11% premium. This would give up a minor part of the potential downside profit for complete upside safety, and whether to take such a step would be a matter of judgment. If one felt the market to be dangerously "toppy" and more likely to move to the downside than the upside, then one could accept that very small upside risk and take the full 100% Hedge.

The Flexibility of the Convertible Hedge

Returning now to the discussion of *"The Most Important Contribution of the Convertible,"* on previous pages, let us recall that the minimized risk of the well-situated Convertible permits us, on the one hand, to take more aggressive advantage of a bottoming-out bear market, so that persisting fear and the resultant timidity do not prevent us from sharing in the typically large percentage advances of the initial market turn. And, on the other hand, the same advantages of the well-situated Convertible permit us to continue to share in the upper reaches of an advanced bull market while guarding against a sudden turn to a bear market. For if there is a sudden and swift turn to descending markets we have demonstrated that loss to invested capital is typically far less in a carefully-selected Convertible than in the respective common stock.

How much more true this is when utilizing the Convertible Hedge! Where we demonstrated common stocks falling twice as fast as their Convertibles in many instances, showing the Convertible position suffering less than half the percentage loss of the common stock, Convertible "arithmetic" when applied to the same examples used showed 0 loss with a Convertible Half-Hedge.

Thus, we gave the example of Belden Corp. 8s of 1990 declining only 11.1% in the drastic November 1972 - August 1973 decline, where the Belden Corp. common stock showed a 24.5% decline in exactly the same period. Undoubtedly it was gratifying to show less than half the loss in the Convertible than for the common stock, but on a later page we described a Convertible Half-Hedge for the same Belden Corp. Convertible Bond and common stock in exactly the same time period, and utilizing *this* Convertible approach reduced the downside loss *to about the 0 level.*

One might seemingly discern an offsetting advantage for taking the greater risk. After all, an *unhedged* position of

Long x amount of Convertible should show twice the profit on the upside as a Half-Hedge position which gives us only a 50% net Long position on the upside. But this is far from an unmixed blessing because where utilizing full 50% margin on an unhedged Convertible position would turn the investment into a speculation—a 25% decline in the Convertible producing a 50% loss in your capital when you utilize full margin—utilizing full margin in a *Convertible Half-Hedge* is much more justified because of the very large degree of downside protection against net loss, as we have demonstrated. This point is important in ways we will now describe, so back to our XYZ Convertible Bond example.

Recapitulating the basic data, each $100 face value of XYZ 6% Convertible Bond is convertible into 2 shares of XYZ common, the Convertible Bond is selling at 100 and the common stock at 50, so the Bond is selling at direct Conversion Parity.

We know that for every point XYZ common rises, the XYZ Convertible Bond must rise 2 points, so each dollar invested in the Convertible Bond must do as well as the same dollar invested in the common stock.

We have agreed (and we have buttressed this agreement with specific examples from the "real world" of Convertibles), that if XYZ common dropped 50% from 50 to 25, the XYZ Convertible Bond would not drop 50% but only by 25%, ceasing its decline around the 75 level. Thus, each dollar invested in the Convertible Bond would show only ½ the loss of the same dollar invested in the common stock.

A Straight "Long" Position

Now consider a straight "Long" position in $10,000 face

amount of XYZ 6% Convertible Bond at 100, with XYZ common doubling in price from 50 to 100.

XYZ Convertibles will rise to *200,* the $10,000 market value will have become $20,000, and each $1 invested will have become $2.

Turning to the downside projection of XYZ common dropping 50% from 50 to 25, the XYZ Convertible Bond will hold up at 75, the $10,000 market value of Bond will have become $7,500 and each $1 invested will have shrunk to 75¢.

A Fully-Margined Unhedged "Long" Position

All the above figures continue to apply, but instead of buying our $10,000 face amount of XYZ 6% Convertible Bonds with $10,000 in cash, we have utilized full 50% margin and have put up only $5,000. With the same upside and downside moves in XYZ common, 50 to 100 on the upside, and 50 to 25 on the downside, our $5,000 cash outlay would still be worth $20,000 on the upside, so each $1 invested would now be $4. So far so good. But on the *down*side, the $2,500 loss when the $10,000 Convertible Bond investment at 100 became worth only $7,500 at 75, represented fully 50% of the original $5,000 investment, so each $1 invested would now be worth only *50¢.*

A Fully-Margined Convertible
HALF-HEDGE Position

Once again, all the above figures continue to apply and we have full 50% margin to carry the $10,000 Long position in XYZ Convertible Bonds, thereby putting up only $5,000. *But,* and without putting up any additional margin, we have taken a Half-Hedge position by selling short 100 shares of XYZ common at 50.

With the same upside and downside moves in XYZ common, 50 to 100 on the upside, and 50 to 25 on the downside, we know from the previous examples of the Half-Hedge position that at 100 for the common and 200 for the Convertible Bond we would have a $10,000 profit in the Convertible Bond and a $5,000 loss in the common short position, for a net $5,000 profit.

This would be only ½ the profit shown by the *unhedged* position using full margin *but* when we look at the downside, with the common slipping to 25, the $2,500 loss representing fully 50% of the $5,000 investment in the fully-margined unhedged position, *now becomes 0 loss with our Half-Hedge.*

A Rational, Prudent Measure Of Risk/Reward Assessment

When you enter into a position in a security where each $1 invested can quadruple on the upside, or be halved on the downside, *you are speculating,* albeit with the odds on your side, and if you place a large amount of funds into such positions, whose loss would be financially significant to you, you are speculating rashly—there is no other way to describe it. Hence, the prudent investor would shun such positions, or, perhaps, involve only a modest amount of funds to "take a flyer."

In a Convertible Half-Hedge position, however, where we have seen that downside exposure of risk is sharply limited and, when well-selected, can be near or at the 0 level, one can rationally, prudently, involve *considerable* funds in seeking upside profits. Therefore, the supposed higher rewards of the unhedged, fully-margined Long position in a Convertible are illusory and the market vehicle of choice in an uncomfortably high market becomes the Convertible Half-Hedge position. And this same reasoning would apply whenever we become concerned about the stock market and about its possible decline.

Thus, consider the end of 1974 following the market disaster of that year. With a potential turn to the upside becoming an ever greater possibility, fear of additional declines was not completely misplaced. Staying on the sidelines a timid, self-defeating approach, and jumping in with large unhedged positions probably foolhardy, the Convertible Half-Hedge approach was perfectly-suited to take advantage of opportunities and sidestep risk to a truly welcome degree.

Utilizing The FULL-Hedge Approach

In a suspiciously "toppy" market, or following an exuberant bull market where there are good reasons for expecting a turn to the downside, the Full-Hedge can come into play to attempt to draw profits from such a conclusion, where one can only gain if one's reasoning is proved correct, and where no loss is possible if one's reasoning proves incorrect. There are few approaches to the always-full-of-danger stock market which can boast of *that* combination of alternatives!

Recall that a Full-Hedge taken in the Belden Corp. 8s of 1990 in November 1972, as fully described on a previous page, produced a 25.77% profit in 9 months, or 34.36% on an annualized basis. And that a similar Full-Hedge established with Occidental Petroleum $3.60 Convertible Preferred, also fully described on a previous page, produced a 30.96% profit in 9 months, or 41.28% on an annualized basis.

With results such as these possible, whenever one is quite uncertain about the near-term direction of the stock market, or whenever one has a conviction that a market spill *is* ahead, a most intelligent approach is to seek out Full-Hedge positions and, indeed, a *combination* of Half-Hedge and Full-Hedge Convertible positions would have the result of hedging against our own convictions. If we were proved *correct,* we would profit from our Full-Hedge positions and suffer small to minimal damage on our Half-Hedge positions. If we were proved *incorrect* by market developments we would suffer minimal to 0 damage on our Full-Hedge positions (depending upon the small premiums in effect when we established the positions) and we would enjoy the profits from our Half-Hedge positions.

Profit-producing *flexibility* is the hallmark of wisely-executed Convertible investment!

Important Income And Tax Advantages Of The Convertible Hedge

"Locking In The Yield"

In our own experience, amazingly few professionals in the securities market, let alone the public investor, take advantage, or are even aware, of this potential benefit of the Full-Hedge which falls into our lap *in addition* to potential downside profits.

We can go back to one of the first pages of this book in explaining this concept of "Locking in the yield," which is actually our own 25-year-old devised name for the process, so quotation marks are necessary. Those first pages described how investors buying Pan American World Airways common stock in April 1975 were literally throwing away a 13.12% yield to no purpose whatever, simply because they were unaware that a Pan American Convertible Bond, the 7½s of 1998, were selling at direct Conversion Parity and were available for purchase.

Let's go back to the applicable figures. Pan American common is selling at 4 and the Pan American 7½s of 1998 are selling at 57⅛. Each $100 face value of Bond is convertible into 14.286 shares of common stock; 4 x 14.286 equals 57.14; the Bond is *selling* at that exact price, at 57⅛; so the Convertible Bond is selling at Conversion Parity.

If we now take a *Full-Hedge* position by buying $10,000 face amount of the Convertible Bond at 57⅛, for $5,712, and selling the full amount of the common stock into which the Bonds can be converted, or 1,428 shares of Pan American common stock, we know:

133

(1) that for any *upside* move of Pan American common stock, the Convertible Bond *must* move up on an equal percentage basis, dollar-for-dollar invested, the gain in the Convertible Bond always completely offsetting the loss via the short-sale in the common stock, *so that no net loss is possible on the upside.*

(2) that for any *downside* move of Pan American common stock, the Convertible Bond portion of the position *cannot* show a greater loss than the offsetting gain on the short-sale of the common, *so that no net loss is possible on the downside.*

If a Full-Hedge taken at Conversion Parity guarantees that no net loss is possible for either an upside or downside move in the common stock, and we know that is mathematically so, then other favorable factors immediately come into the picture as follows:

(1) The 13.12% being earned on the Convertible Bond position is not diminished by any dividend owed on the common stock short position because Pan American common paid no dividend (when you are short a common stock, you *are* debited for any dividends declared on the common stock while you are short).

(2) In a hedged position when you are Long the Convertible and simultaneously short the common stock, we have seen that by Federal Reserve Board margin regulations you need put up no money to carry the short position in the common. Therefore, the 13.12% being earned on the $5,712 invested in the Convertible Bond position accrues completely to the Full-Hedge position.

(3) A no-loss-possible situation puts this Convertible Full-Hedge position, as we see it, in a class by itself where

safety is concerned. Even a government bond, guaranteed as to principal and interest by the United States government, fluctuates in the marketplace so that if you find it necessary to sell the bonds to raise cash, you may find the market value lower than where you made your purchase and suffer a loss. But in a Convertible Full-Hedge position taken at Conversion Parity, the loss in one element of the Hedge must always be completely balanced by the gain in the other element of the Hedge, so that at *any* time, the Hedge position can be liquidated at no possible loss.

(4) The 13.12% yield in this Full-Hedge position *remains* 13.12% whether the common goes up or down—hence it is "locked in"—and no loss is possible on the position, so the safety factor is actually superior to a government bond.

In this particular occasion, with the yield so high, use of full 50% margin in carrying the Convertible Bond is called for, because the margin interest charged by the brokerage house would have to be substantially less than the 13.12% yield on the Bond. Assuming an 8% margin interest rate, this would work out as follows:

The $5,712 needed to purchase $10,000 face amount of the 7½ of 1988 at 57⅛ becomes $2,856 at full 50% margin. Over a one-year period at 8% we would pay $228 in margin charges on the $2,856 borrowed. But we would be receiving $750 in interest on the $10,000 face value at 7½%, so the actual interest income in one year would be $750 minus $228 or $522. On the actual cash outlay of $2,856 to carry the Full-Hedge, this would come to a yield of 18.27%—still on a no-risk basis!

A Special Bonus For Corporate Funds

Having made several references to the surprising lack of knowledge of Convertible opportunities on the part of market professionals as well as public investors themselves, let us add one more: when corporate funds are invested in any stock, common or preferred, *dividends received are 85% forgiven.* The Internal Revenue Service logic on this is that a corporation with a stock investment in another corporation receives a dividend *after* the original corporation has already been taxed on the earnings to produce that dividend. To tax it again to the recipient corporation would be "double taxation" so here is one of the rare expressions of concern about fairness in the weight of taxation. Whatever the reasons, a corporation does report only *15%* of any dividend income received from another corporation for tax purposes, and this can work in quite beautifully with the example we have just described of the Full-Hedge.

Not that this could apply to the examples of Pan American World Airways Convertible *Bonds.* We stated that *dividends* received from a corporation by another corporation are only 15% reportable for income tax purposes, and that does not apply to *bond interest.* Thus, we must turn to a Full-Hedge accomplished with a *Convertible Preferred Stock* to gain this advantage. An example that comes to mind is that of Lykes Youngstown $2.50 Convertible Preferred in late August 1974.

Each share of the Lykes Youngstown $2.50 Preferred Stock was convertible into 1.94 shares of common stock, the common was selling at 10½ and the Convertible Preferred at 21¾. Common price multiplied by Conversion Rate equals Conversion Value, so in this case Conversion

136

Value is 1.94 x 10.50 or 20.37. The premium over Conversion Value is the market price of the Convertible divided by the Conversion Value, so we have 21.75 divided by 20.37 which gives us a minor premium over Conversion Value of 6.7%. At the time the common stock was paying no dividend, while at 21¾ the $2.50 Convertible Preferred was yielding 11.49%.

From this point on, the Convertible arithmetic is exactly the same as we described with Pan American World Airways. A Full-Hedge of Long 100 shares of Lykes Youngstown $2.50 Convertible Preferred Stock and Short the full amount of common stock into which the 100 shares of Preferred could be converted, in this case 194 shares of common stock, could produce only a tiny upside loss (which could be eliminated by taking a 95% hedge instead of a 100% hedge as previously described) at any upside move for the common stock, and could not possibly produce a greater downside loss than the common stock for any move of the common stock in that direction. No loss being possible on either an upside or downside move, this 11.49% yield on the Lykes Youngstown Convertible Preferred was "locked in" with perfect safety—greater safety than for a government bond!

And for corporate funds invested in such a Full-Hedge, the return became remarkable. A fully-taxable return on, say, a corporate bond yielding 11.49% would see 50% (to take a round figure) lost through corporate taxes as straight income, reducing the aftertax yield to 5.74%. Since a corporation reports only 15% of any dividends received from the stock of another corporation, which certainly applies to a Convertible Preferred Stock, the $250 received per annum on 100 shares of Lykes Youngstown $2.50 Convertible Preferred in the Full-Hedge just described, would see only 15% of $250, or $37.50, reported for income tax purposes, of which $18.75 would then be lost to corporate tax. This would leave $250 minus $18.75 or $231.25 in the company's bank account, free of any additional tax, and this would amount to an effective aftertax yield of *10.63%*.

Are we done describing the advantages for such corporate funds investment in the Convertible Full-Hedge? Not quite. Reflecting the near-0 risk of this Full-Hedge position, the use of full margin is called for, so instead of investing $2,175 to carry 100 shares of the Convertible Preferred— nothing at all was required to carry the short position in the common—only 50% of $2,175 need be involved, or *$1,087.*

Recall that when the interest or dividend return on a Convertible is greater than the interest rate charged on margin, the total return goes up. In the case of the Full-Hedge just described with Lykes-Youngstown, taking an average margin rate of 8% would serve to increase the annual return to *15%*. (The $250 per annum dividend is reduced by $87 in margin interest charges, but the $163 in retained dividends is now applicable to a cash outlay of only $1,087.)

Taking advantage of the 85% forgiveness to a corporation of dividend income from other corporations, this would produce an aftertax yield of *12.7%*.

Now, an additional important yield advantage. The interest charged to the corporation for carrying the margin is fully deductible from income. Thus, the $87 in margin interest charged results in a further $43.50 addition to cash

138

flow based on a 50% over-all corporate tax. Since, in computing the 12.7% aftertax yield on a margined basis we had already deducted the full $87 from the $250 in dividend income, we now add back $43.50 to reflect actual cash flow and arrive at an aftertax yield of 19%, "locked-in" and safer than a government bond!

The Downside Profit Potential

In the maze of all the figures above, beneficent as they are, we trust that readers have not lost sight of the fact that in a Full-Hedge taken at Conversion Parity, while no loss is possible on either an upside or downside move for the common stock, the *gain* potential is another, and even more attractive story. On the upside with a Full-Hedge, no loss is possible and no gain is possible. But on the *downside* with a Full-Hedge, to the extent that the Convertible develops a premium over Conversion Value, a net profit will develop on the over-all position. Thus, with our example of the Full-Hedge with Belden Corp. 8s of 1990, described on a previous page, the ability of the Convertible Bond to hold up far better than the common stock on a percentage basis, when the market went into a decline, resulted in a 25.77% net profit in a 9-month period, or 34.36% on an annualized basis.

"Locking in the yield," then, has the potential not only for producing the remarkable risk-free return of a high order that we have described (with the extra benefits for investment of corporate funds), but also has the potential for producing a downside profit which can assume significant dimensions. In the final analysis it is the near-0 or 0 risk of the Full-Hedge taken at or near Conversion Parity that makes what we have just described so valued an approach for any institution, any corporation with funds to invest, any investor.

And the remarkable fact remains that so few investors in any of these categories are aware of these opportunities!

An Impressive Tax Advantage
Of The Convertible Half-Hedge

The Internal Revenue Service holds that when you hedge a Convertible with a short-sale of the common stock, the portion of the Convertible holding that is exchangeable for the amount of common stock sold short does not begin its first day of qualifying for capital gains treatment (more than six-months holding period) until the Hedge is terminated by covering the common short position.

The purpose of this is to prevent a simple and neat maneuver of establishing a number of Full-Hedges at Conversion Parity, which are completely riskless, and then benefiting from those of the Full Hedges which see the common stock go *up* in price. Why would there be a tax advantage? A short-sale by definition is short-term in nature no matter how long it is held. Therefore, in an upside move with a Full-Hedge, while no actual net cash loss or gain is recorded, the loss on the short-side common position is *short-term loss* while, if allowed, the gain on the Convertible would be long-term capital gains if the position were held more than six months.

To eliminate this non-risk tax advantage, *while* the Hedge is in place, the six-month clock cannot begin ticking for the Convertible portion of the position. However, because every *Half*-Hedge Convertible position does encounter risk—that is, when poorly selected, the 2x Convertible portion *can* show greater dollar decline than the x portion of the common stock sold short—the Internal Revenue Service has not, and we do not expect it to because it would be illogical and unjustified, attacked the *unhedged* portion of the Convertible holding in a Convertible Half-Hedge. And this leads us directly to *important* tax advantages.

Back to XYZ 6% Convertible Bonds with each $100 face value of Bond convertible into 2 shares of common stock, and XYZ common selling at 50 and the XYZ Convertible Bond selling at 100, direct Conversion Parity.

We take a Half-Hedge position by buying $10,000 face amount of the XYZ 6% Convertible Bonds at 100 at a cost of $10,000, and selling short one-half the amount of common stock for which the Convertible can be exchanged upon demand, or 100 shares of XYZ common stock.

XYZ common stock doubles from 50 to 100; therefore XYZ Convertible Bonds must be worth a minimum of 100 x 2 or 200.

The $10,000 in face value of XYZ Convertible Bonds is now worth $20,000 for a gain of $10,000.

The short-sale of 100 shares of XYZ common at 50 now shows a 50-point loss for 100 shares or a loss of $5,000.

A gain of $10,000 in the Convertible Bonds, minus a loss of $5,000 in the common stock short-sale, and we have a net gain of $5,000.

The position has been held, say, for 7 months, qualifying for capital gains. As already explained, a short-sale is *always* short-term, no matter how long the position is held. So the loss on the common stock short-sale is a short-term loss. What about the Convertible Bond position? *One*-half of the $10,000 face value, the $5,000 face value portion which could be exchanged for 100 shares of XYZ common stock and which therefore constituted the Hedge portion of the position, remained in a 0-day position for capital gains treatment so long as the common stock short position remained. Therefore, even though held for 7 months and recording a 100% gain, the gain on the $5,000 face-value portion of the Convertible Bond remained a short-term gain.

Since the $5,000 short-term gain on the hedged portion of the Convertible Bond position canceled out the $5,000 short-term loss on the common stock short-sale position, there was no taxable consequence at all for this portion of the position.

What about the $5,000 face value *unhedged* portion of the Convertible Bond? *It* had been held for seven months and unquestionably qualified for capital gains treatment. A $5,000 long-term capital gains profit is chalked up for the holder of this Convertible Half-Hedge position.

Now, recall that when we utilize a low-risk Half-Hedge we are justified in using full 50% margin. We have, therefore, put up $5,000 to carry the Convertible Bond position and nothing at all to carry the common stock short-sale. When XYZ common doubled in price from 50 to 100 and the XYZ Convertible Bond also doubled in price from 100 to 200, and a $5,000 net gain ensued, the $5,000 profit was long-term capital gain, but applicable now *to only a $5,000 cash outlay.*

A $5,000 investment at low-to-0 risk had produced a $5,000 capital gain in this example, or a 100% return in 7 months. This works out to 171% on an annualized basis. Remember that this return is all *capital gain* and that far from being an exercise in hypotheses, every one of the Half-Hedge examples we have given thus far from actual market developments in these pages can be transposed into the Convertible "arithmetic" just discussed.

The tax advantages of the Convertible Half-Hedge are truly impressive!

The Convertible/Call Option Hedge

The short sale (or "writing") of a Call Option while simultaneously taking a "long" position in a Convertible security of the same company combines large profit potential with minimum exposure to risk so effectively that no investor should be without thorough knowledge of the elements going into this approach to market profits. A few definitions to begin with.

The Call Option

A *Warrant,* as distinguished from a Call Option, is issued by the company itself, and is part of its capitalization, representing the right to buy a specific amount of the company's common stock at a specific price, for a specific period of time, the duration of the exercise privilege being almost always for at least a few years, and often for 5, 10 and 20 years. Each *Call Option,* on the other hand, while it is the right to buy (or "Call") 100 shares of a common stock at a specific price, for a specific period of time, is in no way any part of the company's capitalization, and is not issued by the company. Rather does an organized "Option Exchange" set up the trading in the Option contracts, guaranteeing each side of the contract and setting up the all-important "secondary market" where the Option contract can be actively bought and sold throughout the life of the contract.

The greatest difference between the Warrant and the Call Option is also the basis for the profit potential of the Convertible/Call Option Hedge.

Warrants run for *years,* Call Options for *months,* the maximum life of a newly-trading class of Call Options being, typically, about nine months.

The Premium On A Call Option—A "Wasting" Asset

Let's assume an "August 40" Call Option on XYZ Corp., selling at 4 in early-April, so that there are about five months of life remaining for the Option. XYZ common is selling at 38, so the entire $4 price of the Call Option is *premium*. If XYZ Corp. common fails to sell above $40 by August expiration, the entire $4 value of the Option will disappear, become zero, and in order to be *worth* $4 by expiration date, XYZ common must sell at *44*.

If you were bearish on the general market and/or XYZ common, you could sell the XYZ August 40 Call Option short at 4 with the following possibilities:

(1) XYZ common stayed below 40 at the time of August expiration, so you gained the entire $400 you had received when you sold the Option short at 4.

(2) XYZ common sold at 44 at the August expiration date, so you were exactly even because the Call Option you had sold short at 4 had *a market value* of 4 at expiration.

(3) XYZ common sold *higher* than 44 at the August expiration date, in which case you had a loss, the size of the loss determined by how much higher than 44 XYZ common was selling. Thus, if XYZ common sold at *48*, the August 40 Call Option had a value of *8*, and since you had sold short at *4*, your loss was $400 on each Option.

Consider the "numbers" involved here at the start of the various transactions. XYZ common was selling at 38 and the XYZ August 40 Call Option at 4.

To show a profit of $400, XYZ common need only stay below 40 and it could even advance 2 points from 38 to 40 before reducing the $400 profit by one cent.

To show an equal *loss* of $400 from the short sale of the Option, XYZ common must advance to *48,* as we have just seen.

Assuming there were equal chances for XYZ common to go either up or down, we must conclude that it is expecting much more from a stock to go from 38 to 48 in 5 months than it is to simply stay where it is, or decline moderately. One could easily conclude from this analysis that the short-selling of the XYZ August 40 Call Option at 4 had much better odds in its favor of *making* money than losing money, and it would be this writer's feeling that such a conclusion, averaged out over a period of time, was undoubtedly correct.

But there is still the *possibility* of a strong upside run in XYZ common, producing a large loss. Thus, if XYZ common ran to *60,* before the August expiration date, the August 40 Call Option would be worth 20, and the short sale at 4 would show a 16-point loss. How to gain that 4-point premium in the Call Option *without* running that large risk. Is there a way? There certainly is, and let us first point out that the short sale of the Call Option at 4 as thus far discussed is called a "naked short" because the seller owned no common stock. If one owned, or simultaneously purchased, 100 shares of XYZ common stock at the same time the August 40 Call Option was sold short at 4, the "arithmetic" would become very different.

On the *upside,* a $400 to $600 profit is "locked in" because whatever upside level the common reaches, there must be a net $600 profit (slightly less if the common stock is between the 38-40 level on expiration date).

Thus, assume XYZ common reaches *48.* The 100 shares

of XYZ common already held or purchased at 38 show a profit of *$1,000*. At 48, the August 40 Call Option has a value of *8,* and having been sold short at *4,* there is a $400 loss on the short sale.

A profit of $1,000 on the common, and a loss of $400 on the Call Option, and you have a net gain of *$600.*

And at any upside price for XYZ common, at 40 or better, you will always end up with the same result of a $600 net profit.

On the *down*side, the $400 received when you sold the August 40 Call Option short at 4 would enable your 100 shares of XYZ common to fall in the marketplace from 38 to *34* before any net loss would begin to develop, but after that a loss *would* develop. Thus, assume XYZ common plummeted to *30.* You would have a $400 profit on the short sale of the August 40 Call Option at 4, but now you have a loss of $800 from the decline in your 100 shares of XYZ common from a market price of 38 to one of 30. You have a net loss of $400.

The odds, as we see it, still are very favorable for the investor taking the above position because at 4 for the XYZ August 40 Call Option and 38 for XYZ common, a position of Long 100 shares common, short 1 August 40 Call Option would see a $600 net profit if XYZ common rose only 2 points to 40 by the August expiration date, while to generate a similar $600 *loss,* XYZ common would have to fall *10* points from 38 to 28. Quite a difference!

Enter The CONVERTIBLE/Call Option Hedge

In the calculations just described, what is the effect when, instead of a *common stock* long position to offset the Call Option short, we substitute a *Convertible Bond* or a *Convertible Preferred Stock?*

The answer is immediately at hand when we consider that the only threat to the well-situated Long common stock/ Short Call Option Hedge position is an inordinate fall in the common stock. It is the ability of the well-selected Convertible to show less percentage decline than the common stock on the downside, often *far* less percentage decline, that tips the balance even more favorably for the short-seller of the Call Option.

Let's describe an actual example.

It was late-May 1975 and Gulf & Western common was selling at 35⅞ with one of its Convertible Bonds, the 5¼'s-'87, selling at 85½. Since each $100 face value of Bond was convertible at the time (there was a later 2-for-1 split which

---

The publisher, R.H.M. Press, has agreed to make available to the reader, at no extra charge, a Special Supplement, giving the author's current and completely updated analysis and statistical presentation of the entire list of currently outstanding Convertible Bonds and Convertible Preferred Stocks, including a statistical presentation of Euro-Convertible Bonds and Convertibles with Call Option Hedge Potential, in accordance with the description of these areas of "Opportunities In Convertibles" set forth in this book.

To receive this Special Supplement, important to following current opportunities, send your name and address—be sure to include zip—to:

R.H.M. Press Dept. 85
840 Willis Avenue
Albertson, Long Island
New York 11507

There will be no charge for this Special Supplement.

has no effect on any of the calculations which follow) into 2.308 shares of common stock, the straight Conversion Value was 35.875 x 2.308, or 82.80, and the Bond was actually selling at 85½ for a minor 3.2% premium, so that the Convertible was selling quite close to Conversion Parity.

Assume one purchased $13,000 face amount of the 5¼'s-'87 at 85½ for a total investment of $11,115 and sold short the equivalent in January 35 Call Options at 6¼. Since $13,000 face value of Bonds are convertible into about 300 shares of Gulf & Western common, the short sale of the 3 Options fully hedges the position.

Upon making the short sale of the Call Options we would receive 3 x $625, or $1,875. The Hedge position virtually eliminating risk, as we shall soon see, we would use the full 50% margin available and put up $5,557 for the purchase price of $11,115 for the $13,000 face value of Bond. Deducting the $1,875 received for the sale of the Options, our actual cash outlay in this Hedge position would be *$3,682.*

Let us first consider what we would be looking for on the *down*side. At the 1975 low of 23½ for Gulf & Western common, the straight Conversion Value of the 5¼'s-'87 was 23.5 x 2.308, or *54.23,* but the actual 1975 low for the Convertible Bond was *72.* Assuming a return to the lows for common and Convertible Bond, the Bond would drop from 85½ to 72, or 13½ points, and on $13,000 face value, this would be a loss of *$1,755.* Since the January 35 Call Options would have 0 value at 23½ for the common (or *anywhere* below 35 when expiration date of the Option had arrived), the $1,875 received for the short sale of 3 Call Options would more than balance out the $1,755 loss resulting from the decline in the Convertible Bond.

Assessment of downside risk, therefore, in the Convertible/Call Option Hedge just described? Zero, or very close to it, in this writer's opinion, in the market climate of mid-1975.

Examining now what happens when Gulf & Western common moves *up,* it is obvious that only a profit can ensue. As the common stock moves up, the Call Option will also move up, increasing in intrinsic value. *But so will the Convertible move up,* since it is only slightly above straight Conversion Value. And as expiration day for the Call Option approaches, the really important part of the profit potential in such a Convertible/Call Option Hedge begins to come into play, that part being the gradual disappearance of the premium originally being paid for the Call Option at the time the Hedge position was instituted.

Suppose, for example, Gulf & Western common, in the example just cited, would move up to sell at 45 just prior to the January 1975 expiration date of the Call Option. At 45, the January 35's would have a market value of 10, and that is where it would sell directly before expiration. The Call Options having been sold short at *6½,* the price of *10* would mean a loss of 3½ points per Option for a total loss of $1,050 for the 3 Options.

But at 45, the Convertible 5¼'s-'87 must sell at least at 45 x 2.308, or *103.86.* The $13,000 face value of Bond purchased at 85½ for $11,115 are now worth $13,501 with the Bond at 103.86. This profit of $2,386, when we deduct the loss of $1,050 on the short sale of the Options, leaves a net profit of $1,336. Let us also keep in mind that during all of this time the Bonds had a yield of 6.14%, which would be almost enough to offset the interest charge on the 50%

margin used. The above calculations would remain approximately in effect no matter how high Gulf & Western common moved.

Profit And Loss At The Extremes—And In The Middle

With the above calculations we have been demonstrating that with the Convertible/Call Option Hedge, as described, if Gulf & Western common had dropped back to its 1975 *low,* the gain on the short sale of the Call Options would have balanced out the loss in the Convertible as it too dropped back to its 1975 low, with any downside risk then very close to, or at, zero. Any large move to the *upside* for Gulf & Western common would produce a profit of $1,336. (We are ignoring commissions throughout for sake of clarity.) Now, this profit must be considered against the total cash outlay previously calculated as follows: 50% of $11,115, or 5,557 (using the full 50% margin to carry the Convertible Bonds), minus the $1,875 received upon selling the 3 Gulf & Western January 35's short at 6½. This makes the total cash outlay $3,682 and the gross *$1,336* profit calculated above for the upside move comes to a 36.28% profit for the 8-month life of the Option, or about *54%* on an annualized basis. And keep in mind that the Hedge position we have described is close to 0 risk, the only element of risk involving a decline in the Convertible 5¼'s-'87 considerably *below* the old 1975 low. While such could, of course, happen from time to time, the holding power of Convertibles on the downside does not ordinarily go through such radical changes in an eight-month period, and *averaging out* the expectations for the Convertible/Call Option Hedge over a period of time, and with commitments properly diversified over a number of such positions, the designation of "close to 0 risk" as we have described it is, in our opinion, quite accurate.

Finally, in the above calculations, we have treated of prices for Gulf & Western common considerably above, and considerably below the 35⅞ starting price, in order to arrive at profit and loss estimates. Obviously, there is also the large possibility that as expiration day approached, Gulf & Western common would be selling in the same area as when the Hedge position was taken. Thus, assume Gulf & Western common selling at the same 35⅞ price where we initiated our Hedge position at expiration. There would, presumably, be little change in the Convertible long position, but the Option might be selling for, say, 1¼ with a month still to go, producing a 5-point profit on each of the 3 Options, or a gross profit of *$1,500*. Accepting such a profit after 7 months, on the $3,682 cash outlay, would represent a 40.74% profit in that period of time, or a 70% profit on an annualized basis.

The Large Potential Of The
Convertible/Call Option Hedge

What we have described with the Gulf & Western Convertible Bonds and the Gulf & Western Call Options can evolve with *any* Convertible/Call Option price relationship where (a) the Convertible is selling close to Conversion Parity, (b) the Convertible is close to a point where it will begin to strongly resist further decline even if the common stock goes in the downside direction, and (c) there are substantial premiums being paid for a Call Option on the applicable common stock. A quick means of determining whether an opportunity is present is to check to see where the Convertible ceased to decline during the 1975 lows, and how many Call Options could be sold short against a specific amount of Convertible in the long position. If the total to be received upon the short sale of the Call Options about equals the anticipated loss in the Convertible if it fell back to its former lows, we know we are exposed to very little net risk of loss on the downside. Our next step would be to calculate the potential *upside* profit where we would capture the premium being paid for the Call Option, and the calculations should be made precisely as we have done with Gulf & Western in the preceding paragraphs.

Our objective now should be to get the Convertible position past the six-month mark so that it is *all* taxable on a long-term capital gain basis, while keeping the hedged loss in the Call Options sold short *below* the six-month period. This is in no way difficult! With the common stock running to the upside to produce our Convertible profit and our Call Option loss, premiums on new classes of Options at higher price jumps should be considerable.

Thus, assume five months have passed since we first instituted our Convertible/Call Option Hedge in Gulf & Western as just described. It is now late-October and we find a Gulf & Western April 50 Call Option selling at 5 (with the stock at 45, recall). We cover our short of the two original January 35s, establishing our short-term loss, and simultaneously sell 2 April 50s at 5, receiving $1,000 for such sale.

We now have plenty of upside and downside protection all over again to enable our five-month profit in the Convertible to move over into the six-month capital gain area, and we even have the potential for further enhancing our over-all profit. But that would be more a subject for a complete book on Call Options rather than Convertibles, so we will not be carrying the Hedge "arithmetic" further at this point.

What should be obvious, by this time is the *large* measure of profit potential in the Convertible/Call Option Hedge, and with sharply diminished risk potential as well, so that no intelligent investor should ignore this facet of the Convertible. In the back of the book we reprint (courtesy of the R.H.M. Convertible Survey which updates this list in every weekly issue) a list of those Convertibles where Call Options are also trading. With many new Convertibles coming on the scene as we write, and many new Call Options also beginning trading for common stocks not previously covered, the number of potential opportunities in this field have only one way to go—up.

A Most Favorable Aspect Of The
Convertible/Call Option Hedge

In our previous analysis of the Convertible Half-Hedge we explained the quite favorable effect of one-half the Convertible holding being available for capital gains treatment if the position were held for more than six months. The other half of the Convertible position was *not* so available because of an Internal Revenue Service ruling that to the extent that a Convertible Long position was balanced out by a common short-sale, the long-term capital gain clock could not begin ticking until the Hedge was terminated by the covering of the short position. *This is not so with the Convertible/Call Option Hedge.* Even though the short-sale of the Call Options is very effectively acting as a Hedge, the Call Options are not considered to be in the same class as common stock (indeed they are not, by any stretch of the imagination) and the *entire* Long position in the Convertible would be considered as long-term capital gain if the position were held for more than six months and an upside move takes place.

The likelihood of such positions exceeding six months is rather strong, since the largest and most attractive Call Option premiums are typically associated with those Options with the greatest period of exercise life still remaining.

Going back to our example of Gulf & Western Convertible Bonds, with an upside move of the common from 35⅞ to 45 automatically producing a similar move in the Convertible 5¼ s of 1987 from 85½ to 103.86, we estimated a profit in the Convertible position of $2,386. After deducting the hedge part of the loss, $1,050 in the Call Options sold short, we still had a net profit of $1,336 which worked out to a 54% annualized profit.

But in addition now, we must consider that the $2,386 profit in the Convertible Bond position itself was a long-term capital gain because it had been held longer than six months. Once again, the proper strategy in most cases would be to cover the Hedge position in the original Call Options before their six-months holding period was up, to ensure that they would be short-term losses, and to replace them with the short-sale of two longer-lived Call Options. In addition to paving the way for very possibly additional over-all profits on the position, this would enable the entire profit in the Convertible portion of the Hedge position to swing over into the over-six-months holding period for welcome long-term capital gains.

The Convertible/Call Option Hedge has truly remarkable profit potential and as the number of important Convertibles climb (U.S. Steel is selling a large issue of Convertible Bonds, its first Convertible issue in decades, as we go to press) and as the number of common stocks with Call Options trading expands (U.S. Steel, for example, does have Call Options trading actively), these profit opportunities can only increase in number and in scope.

Summing Up

Each trading day, about one thousand Convertible Bonds and Convertible Preferred Stocks, and their respective common stocks, move independently in price from one another, yet also show an intimate relationship.

These ever-changing relationships have a multitude of meanings which can be translated into stock market profits of a high order, probably even greater than we have been able to describe in this book. For Convertibles, wisely selected, intelligently used, can confer one favor above all— *sharply reduced risk,* while allowing generous profits to flow.

Within that risk-reduced environment, so much more money can be put to work seeking profits than can be prudently allotted to common stocks that final results in the Convertible sphere have an excellent chance of towering above those other sectors. Consider, for example, a market which has had a strong advance, with the market now coming to a pause and beginning to move sideways. Professionals and investors alike knit their brows and worry. Is the advance over, and a downside leg now in the offing? Or is this just the prelude to an even stronger upsurge?

Decisions will be made, and the consequences will be enjoyed or suffered. Some investors will extend their common stock holdings, becoming heavily committed, only to see a subsequent market decline producing substantial losses. Others will let timidity and fear rule, liquidate much of their common stock holdings, and then count their missed profit opportunities as a strong market advance gets under way. A succession of "zigging" when you should be "zagging" and "zagging" when you should be "zigging" saps confidence, impairs judgment and further downgrades investment results.

157

How much better it is when you can "read" the meanings of Convertible and common price movement and, as we described in the preceding chapters, find many vehicles among the 1,000 Convertibles trading with which to establish positions where, if a strong move is indeed ahead, you will share in it to a very substantial degree. And if, instead, a market decline is ahead, your invested capital will show far less loss than if your funds had been in the respective common stocks.

Going further, a willingness to look even more deeply into Convertible potential can allow one to establish hedged positions where risk is even more sharply reduced, permitting still larger commitment of funds and the consequent ability to share in upside markets in a leveraged manner, while the unexpected onset of a falling market inflicts only minor damage at a time when other investors, who have not used the Convertible potential, are suffering large losses.

Moving ahead still further, the same Convertible logic can permit one to turn all these factors around to profit from a *falling* market with the same built-in powerful safety factors.

"Locking-in-the-yield" to turn a speculative Convertible into the equivalent of a short-term Treasury note (!), sharply improving the already-promising Common/Call Option Hedge by using a well-situated *Convertible* instead of the common, embracing superior yields and lower commission costs, aiming at substantial tax benefits—*all* of these profit-filled procedures are at the very fingertips of any investor willing to make the effort to understand and use the Convertible.

It is our hope that this book will have served to awaken the interest of the reader to *make* that effort. The rewards can be great because even in this rather extensive study we have only touched on what is possible with the market logic of the Convertible as, every trading day, 1000 Convertibles and their respective common stocks create profit opportunity after profit opportunity, in almost unlimited variety.

We trust this last sentence of this book is a *beginning* for the reader in his interest in Convertibles, not an ending.

A Listing of Publicly-Trading Convertible Bonds

AMF Inc.
ARA Services Inc.
A-T-O Inc.
Aberdeen Mfg.
Advanced Mem. Sys.
Air Reduction
Alaska Airlines
Alaska Interstate
Alexanders Inc.
Alison Mtge. Inv. Tr.
Allegheny Airlines
Allegheny Beverage
Allegheny Ludlum
Allen Group Inc.
Allied Artists Ind.
Allied Stores
Allied Supermkts.
Altec Corp.
Aluminum Co. of Am.
Amerace Corp.
American Air Filter
American Airlines
American Gen. Mtge.
Amer. Cont. Homes
Amer. Export Ind.
Amer. Financial
Amer. General Ins.
Amer. Hoist & Derr.
Amer. Hospital Supp.
Amer. Int'l. Group
Amer. Medicorp Inc.
Amer. Motor Inns
American Motors
Amer. Pipe & Const.
Amer. Realty Trust
Amer. Reserve Corp.
Amer. Safety Equip.
Amfac Inc.
Ampex Corp.
Apache Corp.
Apco Oil Corp.
Applied Data Res.
Arlen Rlty. & Dev.
Armour & Company
Armstrong Rubber
Arwood Corp.
Ashland Oil Inc.
Atico Mtge. Inv.
Avco Corp.
Baird & Warner
Baltimore & Ohio

Bancal Tri-State
Bangor Punta
Bankamer. Rlty. Inv.
Bank of New York
Bank of Virginia
Barber-Greene
Barnett Mtge. Tr.
Barnett-Winston Inv.
Bartell Media
Baxter Travenol
Baystate Corp.
Beaunit Corp.
Becton Dickinson
Beech Aircraft
Belco Petroleum
Belden Corp.
Bell Industries
Beneficial Std. Mtge.
Berkey Photo
Black & Decker
Bliss & Laughlin
Bobbie Brooks Inc.
Bohack, H. C.
Brunswick Corp.
Budd Company
Bulova Watch Co.
Burlington Ind.
Burlington Northern
Buttes Gas & Oil
CMI Investment
Cablecom-General
Cabot Cabot & Forb
Calif. Computer
Capital Mtge. Inv.
Capital Reserve
Carolina Tel. & Tel.
Carrier Corp.
Castle & Cooke
Caterpillar Tractor
Cavanagh Commun.
Ceco Corp.
Celanese Corp.
Cenco Inc.
Centennial Corp.
Central Hud. G & E
Central Tel. & Util.
Cessna Aircraft
Champion Paper
Charter Bnkshs.
Chase Manhattan
Chase Manh Mtge.

Chelsea Industries
Chemical N. Y. Corp.
Chock Full O'Nuts
Chris-Craft Ind.
Circle K Corp.
Citicorp
Citizens & Sthn. S.C.
City Investing
Cluett Peabody
Colorado Nat'l. Bnk.
Columbia Pictures
Combined Ins. Am.
Commonwealth Oil
Computer Sciences
Condec Corp.
Conn. Gen'l. Mtge.
Consol.Leasing Am.
Consol. Oil & Gas
Continental Air Lns.
Continental Mtge.
Continental Tele.
Control Data
Cooper Labs.
Copperweld Steel
Crane Company
Crescent Corp.
Crocker National
Crystal Oil Co.
DPF Inc.
DWG Corp.
Dart Industries
Dasa Corp.
Dataproducts Corp.
Dayco Corp.
Deere & Company
Del Monte Corp.
Devel. Corp. of Am.
Di Giorgio Corp.
Dillingham Corp.
Diversified Ind.
Diversified Mtge.
Dixilyn Corp.
Duplan Corp.
Duro-Test
EAC Industries Inc.
E G & G Inc.
E-Systems Inc.
Eastern Air Lines
Eckerd Jack Corp.
Economics Lab.
EDO Corp.

El Paso Company
Electro Audio Dyn.
Electro-Nucleonics
Electronic Assoc.
Elgin National Ind.
Empire Gas
Engelhard Min. & Ch.
Equitable Life Mtge.
Essex International
Esterline Corp.
Ethan Allen Inc.
Evans Products
Exchange Bancorp.
FMC Corp.
Fairchild Industries
Fairmont Foods
Farah Mfg. Co.
Fedders Corp.
Federal Nat'l. Mtge.
Federal Pac. Elec.
Fibreboard Corp.
Fidelity Corp. Va.
Filmways
First Bank System
First Commerce
First Financial
First & Merchants
First Mortgage Inv.
First Nat'l. Bancrp
First Nat'l. Bk. Atl.
First Nat'l. City Bk.
First Penn Mtge. Tr.
First Realty Inv.
First Union Corp.
First Un. Nat'l. Bnc.
First Un. R E E Mtg.
Fischbach & Moore
Fischer & Porter
Fisher Foods Inc.
Fisher Scientific
Flexi-Van Corp.
Florida Gas Co.
Florida Power Corp.
Ford Motor Credit
Foremost Dairies
Foremost-McKesson
Forest City Enter.
Forest Oil Corp.
Franklin Rlty. & Mtg.
Frontier Airlines
Fruehauf Corp.
G. F. Bus. Equip.
Gates Learjet Corp.
Gelco Corp.

Gen'l. Am. Transp.
Gen'l. Educ. Services
Gen'l. Health Svcs.
General Host
General Instrument
Gen'l. Tel. & Elect.
Georgia-Pacific
Gibraltar Financial
Giddings & Lewis
Girard Trust Bank
Glenmore Distilleries
Godfrey Company
Gordon Jewelry
Grace, W. R. Co.
Granite City Steel
Graphic Controls
Great Amer. Mgmnt.
Great North Nekoosa
Green Giant
Greyhound Computer
Greyhound Corp.
Grolier Inc.
Grow Chemical Corp.
Grumman Aircraft
Grumman Corp.
Gulf & Western Ind.
HNC Mtge. & Realty
Hammermill Paper
Hanover Sq. Realty
Harman International
Harrahs
Harris Tr. & Savings
Havatampa Cigar
Hawaiian Electric
Heitman Mtge. Inv.
Hercules Inc.
Heublein Inc.
Hi-G Inc.
Hills Supermkts.
Hilton Hotels
Hoerner Waldorf
Host International
Hotel Investors
Houston Lt. & Pwr.
Houston Oil & Min.
Humana Inc.
Husky Oil of Dela.
Hyatt Corp.
Industrial Nucleon.
Inflight Services
Insilco Corp.
Instrument Systems
Int'l. Min. & Chem.
International Paper

International Silver
Int'l. Tel. & Tel.
Interstate Bakeries
Interstate Stores
Inv. Diversified Svc.
Ipco Hospital Supp.
Itel Corp.
Jetronic Industries
Jim Walter
Jostens Inc.
Kaman Corp.
Keyes Fibre
Keystone Steel Wire
Kirsch Company
Kresge, S. S.
LTV Corp.
Land Resources Pa.
Leisure Technology
Lincoln American
Lincoln Mtge. Inv.
Litton Industries
Lockheed Aircraft
Lomas & Nettleton
Lone Star Industries
Lucky Stores
MGIC Investment
MacDonald, E. F.
Macke Company
Macmillan Inc.
Macy, R. H.
Madison Sq. Garden
Mallinckrodt Inc.
Management Assist.
Mfrs. Nat'l. Bk. Det.
Marcor Inc.
Maritime Fruit
Martin Marietta
Maryland Cup Corp.
Massmutual Mtge.
McCrory Corp.
McCulloch Oil Corp.
McDonnell Douglas
McGraw-Hill
McKeon Construc.
Median Mtge. Inv.
Medusa Portland
Melville Corp.
Memorex Corp.
Meyer, Fred Inc.
Mid-Continent Tel.
Midland Mtge. Inv.
Midland Resources
Miles Laboratories
Missouri Pacific

Modular Computer
Mohawk Data Scien.
Mony Mtge. Inv.
Morgan, J. P. Co.
Mortgage Inv. Wash.
Nat'l. Bank of Det.
National Can
National Cash Reg.
National City Lines
Nat'l. Dist. & Chem.
Nat'l. Equip. Rental
Nat'l. Health Enter.
National Homes
National Industries
National Kinney
Nat'l. Medical Ent.
Nat'l. Starch & Ch.
New Engl. Mer. N.B.
N. J. Bank & Trust
Newhall Land & Fm.
Nortek Inc.
North Am. Philips
Northeast Airlines
Northern Ind. P. S.
Northrop Corp.
Nthwstn. Mut. Life
OKC Corp.
Oak Industries
Occidental Petrol.
Offshore Company
Ogden Corp.
Old Stone Mtge. Rlty.
Omega-Alpha Inc.
Oneida Ltd.
Optical Scanning
Outlet Company
Owens-Illinois
Ozark Airlines
Ozite Corp.
Pan Amer. Bnkshs.
Pan Am World Air.
Papercraft Corp.
Parker-Hannifin
Penn-Dixie Ind.
Pennsylvania Co.
Pennsylvania Eng.
Pennzoil Company
Pennzoil La. & Tex.
Pepsico
Pepsi Cola
Permaneer Corp.
Pettibone Corp.
Pfizer Inc.
Phillips-Van Heusen

Phoenix Steel Corp.
Piedmont Aviation
Pioneer Texas Corp.
Pittston Company
Pizza Hut
Plessey Co. Ltd.
Punta Gorda Isles
Purex Corp.
Quotron Systems
RCA Corp.
RLC Corp.
Ralston Purina
Ramada Inns
Ranchers Explor.
Reading & Bates
Realty & Mtg. Pac.
Realty Income Tr.
Reeves Brothers
Republic Mtge. Inv.
Republic Nat'l. Bk.
Restaurant Assoc.
Revere Cop. & Br.
Rexnord Inc.
Reynolds Metals
Richford Industries
Riegel Textile
Roblin Industries
Rochester Tele.
Rockwell Int'l.
Rohr Industries
Rusco Industries
Rust Craft Greeting
Ryan Homes
SCM Corp.
St. Regis Paper Co.
Sanders Associates
Sanitas Service
Santa Fe Industries
Santa Fe Internat'l.
Saul, B. F. REIT
Seaboard World Air.
Seatrain Lines Inc.
Sherwin-Williams
Sinclair Oil Corp.
Skil Corp.
Society Corp.
Sola Basic Ind.
Solitron Devices
Sonderling Bdcstg.
Southeast Banking
Southern Airways
So. Calif. Edison
Spector Industries
Sperry Rand Corp.

Sprague Electric
Standard-Pacific
Standard Packaging
Std. Prudential
Standex Int'l.
Stanwood Corp.
Sta-Rite Industries
State Mutual Inv.
State St. Bk. & Tr.
Stevens, J. P.
Storer Broadcstg.
Suave Shoe Corp.
Sun Electric
Sundstrand
Sunshine Mining Co.
Susquehanna Corp.
Sutro Mtge. Inv. Tr.
Sybron Corp.
Talcott National
Tappan Company
Technical Oper.
Technical Tape
Tenneco Inc.
Tenneco Offshore
Tesoro Petroleum
Texfi Industries
Texstar Corp.
Tidewater Marine
Trane Company
Trans-Carib. Airl.
Trans-Lux Corp.
Trans-World Airl.
Tri-South Mtge. Inv.
Tyco Laboratories
UV Industries Inc.
Unimax Group Inc.
Union Corp.
Union Pacific Corp.
Uniroyal
United Air Lines
United Brands Co.
United Merchants
United Nuclear
U. S. Bancorp
U. S. Bancorp Rlty.
U. S. Fin. of Fla.
U. S. Home Corp.
U. S. Realty Inv.
U. S. Steel
United Technologies
United Utilities
United Va. Bnkshs.
Util. & Ind. of Del.
VLN Corp.

Vail Associates
Vanadium Corp.
Van Dorn
Vendo Company
Vernitron
Va. Elec. & Power
Wal-Mart Stores
Walgreen Company
Wallace-Murray
Wean United
Welded Tube of Am.

Wells Fargo Bank
West Point-Pepp.
Westcoast Trans.
Western Air Lines
Western Union Corp.
White Consol. Ind.
White Motor
Whittaker Corp.
Wickes Corp.
Will Ross Inc.
Wilshire Oil Co.

Witco Chemical
Wometco Enter.
Work Wear Corp.
Wyle Laboratories
Wyly Corp.
Xerox Corp.
Zapata Corp.
Zapata Exploration
Zayre Corp.
Zurn Industries

A Listing of Publicly-Trading Convertible Preferred Stocks

AMAX Inc.
A-T-O Inc.
Aetna Life & Cas.
Allegheny Beverage
Allegheny Ludlum
Altec Corp.
Amerace Corp.
Amerada Hess Corp.
American Bakeries
American Brands
Amer. General Ins.
Amer. Home Prod.
American Standard
Amer. Tel. & Tel.
Amer. Waterworks
Amstar Corp.
Arcata National
Arizona-Col. Land
Armco Steel Corp.
Arvin Industries
Ashland Oil Inc.
Atlantic City Elec.
Atlantic Richfield
Avco Corp.
Avnet
Baltimore G & E
Bangor Punta
Basic Inc.
Beatrice Foods
Bendix
Beneficial Corp.
Bergen Brunswig
Borden Inc.
Bristol-Myers
Bunker Ramo
CBS Inc.
CIT Financial

CNA Financial
Carter Hawley Hale
Central Securities
Champion Int'l.
Chris-Craft Ind.
Chromalloy Amer.
City Investing
Cluett Peabody
Coastal States Gas
Colt Industries
Combustion Eng.
Commonwealth Ed.
Commonwealth Oil
Consolidated Edison
Consolidated Foods
Consumers Power
Continental Corp.
Continental Oil
Continental Tele.
Cooper Industries
Cooper Tire & Rub.
Crocker National
Crouse-Hinds
Crum & Forster
Cummins Engine
Curtiss-Wright
DWG Corp.
Dart Industries
Dayco Corp.
Dennison Mfg. Co.
Detroit Edison
Diamond Shamrock
Di Giorgio Corp.
Dillingham Corp.
Duke Power Co.
Eagle-Picher Ind.
Eaton Corp.

Elec. Mem. & Mag.
Emhart Corp.
Ethyl Corp.
FMC Corp.
Fairmont Foods
Federal Paper Bd.
First Hartford Corp.
First Va. Bnkshs.
Flickinger, S. M.
Flintkote Co.
Fluor Corp.
Foote Mineral Co.
Foremost-McKess.
GAF Corp.
GATX Corp.
Gamble-Skogmo
General Instrument
Gen'l. Tel. & Elec.
Genesco
Golconda Corp.
Golden West Fin.
Gould Inc.
Green Giant Co.
Gulf & Western Ind.
Gulf Res. & Chem.
Gulton Industries
Heinz, H. J.
Heller, Walter E.
Hesston Corp.
Holiday Inns
Household Finance
Hubbell, Harvey
Hydrometals
IC Industries Inc.
IU International
Ideal Basic Ind.
Indianapolis P & L

Ingersoll Rand
Inland Steel
Insilco Corp.
Instrument Systems
Int'l. Banknote
International Ind.
Int'l. Tel. & Tel.
Interpace Corp.
Iroquois Brands Ltd.
ITT Consumer Svc.
Jim Walter
Johnson Controls
Kaiser Al. & Chem.
Kaiser Cem. & Gyps.
Kaman Corp.
Katy Industries
Kaufman & Broad
Kidde, Walter
Koehring Co.
LFE Corp.
LTV Corp.
Lear Siegler
Lehigh Valley Ind.
Libbey-Owens-Ford
Liberty Loan Corp.
Liggett Group Inc.
Lincoln First Banks
Lincoln National
Lipe-Rollway Corp.
Litton Industries
Lone Star Industries
Long Island Lghtg.
Lykes Corp.
Macmillan Inc.
Marcor Inc.
McGraw-Hill
Mead Corp.
Mercantile Bnkshs.
Mesa Petroleum
Missouri Pacific
Molycorp Inc.
Monsanto Co.
Munford Inc.
NICOR Inc.
National Can Corp.
National Industries
Newmont Mining
Northrop Corp.
Northwest Ind.
Norton Simon
Occidental Petrol.
Ocean Drill. & Ex.

Ogden Corp.
Orange & Rock. Ut.
Owens-Illinois
Pacific Holding
Paine Webber Inc.
Pargas Inc.
Peerless Insurance
Pennsylvania Co.
Pennwalt Corp.
Pennzoil Company
Pet Inc.
Petrolane Inc.
Petro-Lewis Corp.
Philips Industries
Pitney Bowes Inc.
Potomac Elec. Pwr.
Pratt-Read Corp.
Pratt & Lambert
Premier Industrial
Public Svc. of N. H.
Public Svc. N. C.
Puget Sound P & L
Purex Corp.
Quaker Oats
Questor Corp.
RCA Corp.
Rapid-American
Reliance Electric
Reliance Group
Rexnord Inc.
Reynolds Industries
Reynolds Metals
Riggs National Bk.
Rio Grande Ind.
Rockwell Int'l.
Rocky Mt. Nat. Gas
Rohr Industries
Ruddick Corp.
Santa Fe Ind.
Sargent Industries
Savannah El. & Pwr.
Scovill Mfg.
Seaport Corp.
Sheller-Globe
Sherwin-Williams
Signal Companies
Singer Company
Southdown Inc.
Sthn. Cal. Edison
Southern Railway
Sthwest. Forest Ind.
Sperry & Hutchinson

Stud.-Worthington
Sun Company Inc.
Sundstrand
Supermkts. Gen'l.
Susquehanna Corp.
Sybron Corp.
T I M E DC Inc.
TRW Inc.
Talley Industries
Tannetics Inc.
Teledyne
Tenneco Inc.
Tesoro Petroleum
Texas Gas Trans.
Textron Inc.
Total Petrol. Ltd.
Transamerica
Trans World Airl.
Travelers Corp.
UAL Inc.
UV Industries Inc.
Unimax Group Inc.
Union Oil of Calif.
Union Pacific
United Bk. of N. Y.
United Brands
United Industrial
United National
U. S. Gypsum
United Technologies
United Telecommun.
Victor Comptometer
Vulcan Inc.
Wachovia Corp.
Wallace-Murray
Warnaco Inc.
Warner Commun.
Washington Gas
Washington Nat'l.
Wayne-Gossard
Wean United
Western Union
Weyerhaeuser Co.
Whittaker Corp.
Willcox & Gibbs
Williams Cos.
Winn-Dixie Stores
Witco Chemical
Woolworth, F. W.
Zale Corp.
Zapata Corp.

A Listing of Publicly-Trading Euro Convertible Bonds

Address.-Multi.
American Brands
American Can Int'l.
Amer. Exp. Ov. Fin.
Apco International
Ashland Overseas
Beatrice Foods Ov.
Borden Overseas
Chevron Overseas
Chrysler Overseas
Cont. Tele. Int'l.
Dart Industries Inc.
Deere (John) Ov.
Dillingham Int'l.

Eastman Kodak
Firestone Overseas
Fort Int'l. Capital
General Elec. Ov.
Gillette Int'l. Cap.
Gulf & West. Int'l.
Harris Int'l. Fin.
Int'l. Std. Electric
Int'l. Tel.& Tel.
Jonathan Logan Ov.
Kidde, Walter Ov.
LTV International
Leasco Int'l.
Marine Midland Ov.

Miles International
Motorola Int'l. Dev.
Pan Am. Overseas
Penney, J. C. Int'l.
RCA Int'l. Dev.
Revlon Inc.
Searle, G. D. Int'l.
Squibb Int'l. Fin.
Texaco Oper. Eur.
Twent. Cent.-Fox
Union Carbide Int'l.
Ward Foods Ov.
Warner-Lambert
Xerox Corp.

A Listing of Convertibles With Call Options Trading

AMF Inc.
Aetna Life & Cas.
Alum. Co. of Amer.
Amerada Hess
Amer. Home Prod.
Amer. Hosp. Supp.
Amer. Tel. & Tel.
Atlantic Richfield
Avnet
Baxter Travenol
Beatrice Foods
Black & Decker
Brunswick
Burlington Nthn.
CBS Inc.
Caterpillar Tractor
Chase Manhattan
Citicorp
Commonwealth Ed.
Consolidated Edison.
Continental Oil
Continental Tele.
Control Data
Deere & Company
Delta Airlines
Diamond Shamrock
Eastman Kodak
El Paso Company
Engelhard Minerals

Fed. Nat'l. Mtge.
Firestone Overseas
Fluor Corp.
Ford Motor Co.
GAF Corp.
General Electric
Gen'l. Tel. & Elec.
Gillette
Grace, W. R.
Greyhound Corp.
Gulf & Western Ind.
Hercules Inc.
Holiday Inns
Household Finance
Int'l. Min. & Chem.
Int'l. Tel. & Tel.
Jim Walter
Kresge, S. S.
McDonnell Douglas
Mesa Petroleum
Minn. Mng. & Mfg.
Monsanto Co.
Morgan, J. P.
Motorola Int'l.
Nat'l. Cash Register
Nat'l. Dist. & Chem.
Norton Simon
Occidental Petrol.
Penney, J. C.

Pennzoil Co.
Pepsico
Pfizer
RCA
Reynolds Ind.
Santa Fe Int'l.
Searle, G. D.
Sperry Rand
Std. Oil of Calif.
Sun Company
TRW Inc.
Teledyne
Tenneco Inc.
Tesoro Petroleum
Texaco Oper. Eur.
Transamerica
UAL Inc.
Union Carbide
Union Oil of Calif.
United Technologies
Va. Elec. & Power
Warner-Lambert
Western Union
Weyerhaeuser Co.
Williams Cos.
Woolworth, F. W.
Xerox Corp.

The publisher, R.H.M. Press, has agreed to make available to the reader, at no extra charge, a Special Supplement, giving the author's current and completely updated analysis and statistical presentation of the entire list of currently outstanding Convertible Bonds and Convertible Preferred Stocks, including a statistical presentation of Euro-Convertible Bonds and Convertibles with Call Option Hedge Potential, in accordance with the description of these areas of "Opportunities In Convertibles" set forth in this book.

To receive this Special Supplement, important to following current opportunities, send your name and address—be sure to include zip—to:

R.H.M. Press Dept. 85
840 Willis Avenue
Albertson, Long Island
New York 11507

There will be no charge for this Special Supplement.

NOTES

NOTES

NOTES

NOTES

NOTES